Love, WAR, and Glory

Spoken Words
for
All Seasons

DENIS OLASEHINDE AKINMOLASIRE

authorHOUSE®

AuthorHouse™ UK
1663 Liberty Drive
Bloomington, IN 47403 USA
www.authorhouse.co.uk
Phone: 0800.197.4150

Published by AuthorHouse 07/26/2018

ISBN: 978-1-5462-9450-4 (sc)
ISBN: 978-1-5462-9451-1 (hc)
ISBN: 978-1-5462-9449-8 (e)

Contents

Love

A Diamond in the Sky

Stars. Beautiful, aren't they? At night I often lie awake and stare at the sky, hoping for a star to light up my heart. What is it about the stars that makes me wonder? Is it the mystery, is it the fact they are far above, or could it be that they remind me of you? To me, you are a star—the way you sparkle, the way you shine, just like a diamond in the sky.

To me, there is no finer sight than a clear-blue night with nothing but the view of the sky above. A night on the town? I'd rather have a night with the stars. To me, you are a star, a fine sight, and a true wonder of the world, just like a diamond in the sky.

Just like the stars above, diamonds are forever. They never go away. They're always there, ready to be glanced at. All you need is the right time and place, and like you, the stars are a sight to behold. Once I catch sight of you, I know all my troubles will go away. (Well, in your case, sometimes the trouble is about to begin.) For me, you're my special diamond in the sky.

Wonder Woman

Wonder woman. My wonder woman.
There may officially be eight wonders in the world,
but as far as I am concerned,
the only wonder in this world is you.

You're my light, my strength, my guiding angel.
You're the reason I come home at night.
All the ingredients I could want in a woman are in you.
They say that nothing is perfect, but you're as close to perfection as can be.

I have never seen someone so kind, so gentle, yet so humble.
It's amazing how I feel whenever I am with you.
With you I feel that anything is possible.
Whenever I'm sad, you are there to provide me with a smile.

When I need support, you provide me with a rock to stand on.
And most of all, the love you provide is everlasting.
Wonder woman. You're my wonder woman now and forever more.
I really do not want to be without you.

You're my wonder woman for life.

When I Think of You

When I think of you, my heart goes wild.
When I think of you, all my troubles go away.
When I think of you, I feel I can boldly go where no one has gone before.
When I think of you, I feel I can climb mountains.

When I think of you, I know everything is going to be just great.
When I think of you, I feel I am the best.
When I think of you, I feel I can go all the way.
When I think of you, I feel truly invincible; I feel like the "Man of Steel".

When I think of you, I feel like the champ.
When I think of you, I know I'm going to win.
When I think of you, I feel like I'm the best.
When I think of you, I just think, Wow!

When I think of you, my head goes dizzy.
Sometimes when I think of you,
I wonder what I did to deserve meeting someone as special as you.
When I think of you, I think you are beauty at its finest.
When I think of you, I think it's going to be a happily ever after.

Whatever Happened to the Concept of Marriage?

Marriage. Till death do us part. For better and for worse, and for richer and poorer. Marriage is meant to be for life. Why do so many marriages fail these days? Why does no one believe in marriage anymore?

The wedding should be one of the happiest days one can ever have. It should be a joyous occasion. It should be something to aspire to. It should be a day to remember and to finally be at peace and ready to make a commitment to someone for the rest of your life. Getting married should be about finally confirming that you have a partner for life. So the real question is, why do marriages fail?

Why *do* marriages fail? That is a very good question. It is one of life's greatest mysteries. One thing I often hear is that sometimes people change. During twenty, thirty, or forty-plus years with someone, you are definitely going to change as a person. You are going to change physically and mentally. You are going to go through situations you haven't encountered previously. The trick is to go through those changes together. You can't go through them by yourself. It is important to be there for each other and support each other whilst going through those changes.

What about sacrifice? Sacrifice is definitely needed to make a marriage work. When you get married, you have to sacrifice. To a certain degree, your freedom goes. When you're single, you can go as you like and do as you please. You define your own schedule. Marriage isn't about two people being joined at the hip. You can still be you. But it is a question of making time for your partner and letting that person become part of your life. And when deciding, it is about thinking of the implications to your partner and family.

Then there is the wedding day itself. Too often we think about the wedding and not the marriage. They are two different things. The wedding is just one day; marriage is for the rest of your lives. Weddings are not about parents being able to show off or random people coming to the reception just to enjoy their ten different plates of Jollof rice. The real reason for the wedding is two people wishing to commit to each other for the rest of their lives. Of course, we're going to be happy and proud when our children get married. No doubt it should be a celebration. And respect the traditions relevant to your culture, but never ever forget why the wedding is truly taking place. It is about two people who want to be together for the rest of their lives. Never lose sight of that.

Another factor to consider is communication. One of the basic human skills, something we are taught throughout our academic careers, but it is something we have yet to truly master. Communication is vital for a marriage to work. We are not mind readers. We must let our partners know how we feel and not keep everything bottled up inside. When there is a problem, talk it out; figure out what the real root cause is. Communication isn't just about speaking; it's about listening and hearing. Listening is giving your partner a chance to speak. Hearing is about understanding and empathizing with where your partner is coming from. If there is no communication, the marriage will not work.

But do you know what the most important factor is in a marriage? It is not the parents or each other's family. It is not about friends. The most important factor is the two people who got married. Sometimes you are going to argue and do something to offend each other. It is natural; we are only human after all. But never forget why you married your partner in the first place. Never forget what made you two fall in love. Your dating life isn't over when you get married. If anything, it is just beginning. The difference is now you have a lifetime partner to go on dates with. So don't forget to enjoy being together.

It is true that a lot of marriages fail these days. Marriage isn't easy, and there will be challenges. The important thing is to stand by each other. Work on it each day, and reaffirm each other's love for the other. Think about what sort of husband or wife you want to be, and never stop trying to be the best partner you can be. The concept of marriage is still as valid, relevant, and real as it ever was. The question is what you are willing to do to make sure it lasts.

Heartbreak

How did it all come to this? Everything was going so well. No arguments, no clue, no build-up, and a bullet that came out from the blue. After all the things we did. After being so kind to me, being the sweetest person I have ever met. She even came with me to a wedding where she met my mum, and she came to my nephew's birthday party, where she met the rest of my family. Why do all that and call it quits? Leave my heart in tatters. Thanks for nothing.

Even the reason she gave was baffling. Timeline—there was no mention of a timeline when we first started seeing each other. You could have set expectations. There was no timeline when you allowed me to take you to the theatre for your birthday as a surprise. The fact that I had a house. Why is me having a house a problem? I thought women wanted to be with someone who had his head sorted and was making plans for the future. All my friends and family were proud and happy that I had a house, so why it is the woman I loved wasn't?

Even the Christmas present you bought me. Very expensive, and not a gift you simply just go out and buy from Argos. A high-speed driving day gift card of all things. A gift so thoughtful and very inspiring; the sort of gift that screams out that I love you. You do all that and break someone's heart. Why? What on earth where you thinking about? In fact, what were you looking for in the first place? All the heartbreak and pain could have been avoided if you had your head screwed on and knew what you wanted in the first place.

Love is a very powerful emotion. When it works, you are on cloud 9. When it doesn't; it can leave you feeling empty and lonely. What can you do to make this pain go away? Time, patience, and learning to let go. If you can say hand on heart that you did everything right by that person and it

6

didn't work, then it really is a case of you not being the problem. You're not the problem, she is. She missed the boat; she failed to catch the stream. If she can't be happy because of things you've accomplished, she is not worth the time and hassle, and she isn't someone you should have in your life.

You'll find your partner. But take your time. Make sure she or he is right for you. Don't rush. Find out what the person's looking for. Be honest and transparent. You'll know when you've struck gold. Break-ups happen; it's a fact of life. The trick is how you deal with it. That's what really matters. Feel better. Hopefully this has helped.

Perfect

Perfect, just perfect. Perfection; the goal of almost every person on this planet. Everyone wants something to be perfect. The perfect coursework, the perfect exam, the perfect pass, the perfect player; we even want the perfect girl. Why does everything in life have to be perfect?

Look at all the magazine advertising using so-called perfect models and perfect people. Look at the people who criticize something or someone, acting as if they could do better. But guess what? We weren't built to be perfect; we were built to live our lives.

Life isn't meant to be perfect. If it were, it would be terribly boring. Where would our sense of drama come from? Where would the adventure come from? No magic, no passion, no energy. A soulless, predictable life or a life with twists and turns, living on the knife-edge. I know which I would prefer.

So instead of trying to make life perfect, instead of trying to make every little detail go according to plan, let's live a little. Let's have no fear; let's make every move a bold move. We'll get to where we want to be in the end, just not in the way we expected.

The One

I'm looking for someone. Just someone. I'm looking for the one. I'm looking for the one who will complete me. The one who will fulfil me. The one who will love me. The one who will care for me. The one with whom I will build my future. I'm looking for the one.

I'm looking for the one. I'm looking for the final piece of the jigsaw puzzle. I'm looking for the one who will be the cherry on top. I'm looking for the one who will get our title challenge into gear. I'm looking for the one who will kick-start our march to glory.

I'm looking to hire someone. I'm looking for someone to fill a role on my team. I'm looking for someone who will fit into the culture of the firm. I'm looking for someone who will be here for the long haul. I'm looking for the one.

I'm looking for a place to study. I'm looking for somewhere to fulfil my ambitions. I'm looking for a place that will allow me to fulfil my potential and help me fulfil my destiny. I'm looking for that special place. I'm looking for the one.

I need help getting over this final hurdle. I need a teacher. I need someone calm, someone patient. I need someone who can understand me and tell me the truth when I need to hear it most. But in the end, I need someone who I know will have my back. I want that person to be the one.

I'm looking for a leader. Someone who can inspire us. Someone who will lead us into battle. Someone who won't abandon us. Someone who will protect us at all times. I want that someone to be someone I can be proud of. I want that person to be the one.

That's the thing about life. At different stages, we are all looking for someone or something. Sometimes we go to ridiculous means to find it. Sometimes when we think that we have found what we are looking for, we end up disappointed. Disappointment happens in life. That doesn't mean we should stop searching. Perhaps it's how we are searching that needs to be changed.

Whatever it is that you are looking for, you will find it. It may take time. Be patient, be open, and by all means, put yourself out there. However, don't let that search consume you. Relax and let it come. Then and only then will you find what you're looking for. Then the one will come to you. You will find the one.

Just the Two of Us

I remember when I first met you. I was attracted to you immediately. I could not take my eyes off you. It really was love at first sight. It was just us on that romantic night. From the fun we had in the M&M store to the joy we got from the street performers. Despite neither of us being drinkers, we had the bar next door to ourselves. It was a sweet moment. It really was just the two of us.

Me and you have had some special times. Be it our trip to the arts gallery in Kensington, when we surprised each other with our knowledge and passion for ancient history, or our amazement at some of the discoveries we made at the Science Museum. We were learning and growing together. Growing at our own pace and learning in our way, the two of us starting out on this lifelong journey together. The two of us were on this road together.

One of the sweetest things you ever did was organize our trip to Kew Gardens. It was in the middle of autumn. It was still very early in our relationship. We were able to venture into a world that would have made Alice in Wonderland blush. We were able to sit on the bench and admire the beautiful scenery, exchanging our deepest thoughts and sharing the sweetest words without a care in the world. It was a perfect moment. It was just the two of us.

I always remember our first dance together. It wasn't in some nightclub or posh venue. I got my laptop out and played one of my favourite tunes right in the middle of our living room. It wasn't anywhere fancy; it didn't need to be anywhere fancy. It was just us sharing the moment together. It was our moment. It was all just us. It was all about us. It was just the two of us, and on that day, we didn't need anything more.

I still remember all the nights you used to spend on the sofa. I was there, watching the football, and you just fell asleep in my arms. With you in my arms, I always felt like I was lying next to my guardian angel. There was no harm that could come our way. It was just the two of us.

I remember the days when I came home tired after work and training. I was always worrying about the future and how we would position ourselves for what lay ahead. I used to wonder with all the bills and the way property prices were rising, how our future children would be able to prosper in this world. In a world divided by Brexit and Trump, how could we possibly provide the best possible platform for our future children? Yet with you by my side, I never lost faith. I was never alone. We were in this together. The two of us would face this uncertainty together. It really was just the two of us.

Someday it is just going to be the two of us. Our kids will someday leave the nest that is our home and hopefully build lives and families of their own. And when that happens, I will love you as always. I will be with you till the end of the line.

The One Who Makes Me Go Crazy

Life. You only live it once. In your lifetime, you meet all kinds of people. You meet great people, you meet super people, and then you meet people who make you go crazy. And girl, you are the one who makes me go crazy. You are one of a kind.

Girl, you are mad; you are bonkers. You've got the smile, the look; and best of all, you have wonderful hair. (It's true, seriously; look in the mirror.)

Girl, you annoy me like a little sister. But just like my sister, who just wants to get a carry from her brother, you always smile when I'm around (well, in your case, perhaps half the time—if at all).

But girl, you drive me crazy. You make me feel dizzy. You turn my world upside down. I never know what's next when you're around. One minute I'm sad, next I'm angry and about to unleash rage (all right for me; I do that anyway), then all of a sudden, I feel on top of the world.

Girl, you're nuts. You've got the look. There are many wonderful—and annoying—things about you. But most of all, you are the one who makes me go crazy.

A Sight to Behold

"Beauty." A word I don't use very often. When I see you, I can barely take my eyes off you. You have a license to thrill, to stand out like a star. You're a one-in-a-million person. You're a sight to behold.

Your hair is as smooth as silk. (Which is why I keep touching it—LOL!) Your skin is as pure as the elements, your smile makes me buzz like a bee, and the sheer sight of you makes my heart melt like butter. You're a sight to behold.

To me, your guy is a lucky man. I pity the fool who lets you go. (You can laugh now.) If it were me, I'd hold on tight and never let you go. You are like honey to a bear, water to fish; you're magical. You're a sight to behold.

There is not a more beautiful sight than seeing your gorgeous smile and your bright, beaming eyes. That and your great body! For me, you are wonder woman; you are my super girl, a wonder of the world. You're a sight to behold.

Loved Ones

Loved ones. Friends, family, the special people in your life are the ones who know you best. They are the ones who know how to make you smile. They know how to make you laugh, what to do when you're sad, and when best to leave you alone.

Your loved ones will do things for you without you even asking. Why? Because that is what your loved ones will do for you. Your loved ones will provide happiness like none other. To have loved ones is a blessing. Count yourself lucky. Not everyone has them. Cherish them, and grow your love with your loved ones.

Your loved ones will stick their necks out for you. They are the ones who will come to your aid no matter how much trouble you are in. Sometimes they can be taken for granted. Never take your loved ones for granted. Always respect and be there for them.

Your loved ones show unconditional love that is hard to come by. You lose that, you lose a piece of yourself that will be close to impossible to win back. People can forget what you did, but they will never forget how you made them feel. Throwing unconditional love back in someone's face is the equivalent of giving someone the money shot in wrestling. It's a hurtful thing that may be unforgiveable.

Make sure you take care of your loved ones always as they will be with you till the end of the line.

Smile

"Smile"; just one simple word. Just smile. Turn that frown upside down. Something so simple and something we learn how to do from a young age. Then why do we often forget to smile? How did we forget to smile?

At times, life can be cruel and unfair. The world is in a strange place at the moment. We live in a world where we are as divided as ever; Brexit proved that. Despite the progress that has been made, racism still exists in various forms. We live in a world where hunger and slavery still exist. We live in a world where not all of us have access to clean water. Some of us are still starving. The world is not a nice place.

When I get on the tube, I see so many down faces. It's as if going to work is no longer fun. It's as if we are working to live. Shouldn't it be the opposite way around? But why do we make it harder for ourselves? Since when did we become so downtrodden? Since when did we become zombies? Our hearts are still beating; we are still breathing. So come on, everyone, it isn't all bad. I mean seriously, let's smile.

For everything that is bad, let us not forget what is good. I think back to the London 2012 Olympics and the 2017 World Championships. Or Glasgow 2014, when I got to see the great man Usain Bolt in the flesh. It is true that we currently have Trump, but let's not forget about Barack Obama. Who would have thought we would see a black person live in the White House? So let's crack smiles on those faces of ours.

When you're sad and things are down, think back to all the good that you've seen and done in this world. Think back to the times when you were happy. Think about what makes you happy. If you like running, then go for your run. If you want to travel, then by all means, get your passport and go travelling. And when it comes to your kids, remember why you love them. In my case I'm now a book author. If you told me ten years ago that would happen, I would have thought you were absolutely mad. Think back and smile.

We all go through hard times. We all go through periods when things are not going as well as we planned. We go through trials and tribulations. That is the way of life. But no matter how bad it gets for you, just remember there are people out there who have it worse than you. You're still alive and kicking. You can still pursue your goals. You're working, you can travel, and you still have a loving family. So don't forget to smile.

To Love Someone

I love you. Just three simple little words, but three little words with a big meaning. All of us want to be loved. The real issue is how we behave when we love someone. And more importantly, how we behave when someone loves us.

If you love someone and he or she loves you, make sure you do right by that person. Treat the individual well. Make the other person feel as if he or she is the most precious person in the world. Treating them well is not about buying the most expensive gifts. Love isn't about taking them to the poshest places or gallivanting on exotic holidays. That is part of getting to know them and part of the falling in love process. It is the cherry on top of the cake. It is not the main ingredient. Love is about putting another person first. Don't be selfish. Don't just think about what is good for you.

Build together; plan together. Both of you need to combine what you have and build something that is greater than the sum of your parts. Sometimes it's the small things that matter, such as making breakfast, doing the laundry, making the bed, or making sure the other got home safely after a night out. Remember the day and how you first met. It's about understanding what is important to one another and why. In love, it is the small things that matter the most.

Many of us often ask what it means to love someone. I mean, how do you know when you are in love? Love is not something you can define by going off some dictionary definition. It isn't a mathematical formula. You can't predict when or how it will happen. It is about how you feel on the inside when you're with that person. But more important, it is about how you feel when you're not with that person. When you're not with that person, how do you feel? Do you miss that person? Do you feel like a part of you is empty? Do you feel like you're stranded, lost in a sandstorm when separated? Would losing the person devastate you? That's love, and love can hurt.

Love is not always a smooth-sailing journey. There will be lots of challenges along the way. The trick is to be there for each other when your love is tested most. When you have seen each other at your worst and came out the other side, what else do you have to fear? It's easy to be happy when things are going well, but what about when things aren't going well? Setbacks can happen. When you come through those moments, your love is tested and is stronger for it. When you have passed this stage, then and only then do you know you're onto something unbreakable.

The other thing is why do you love the other person? Is it because of her beauty? Is it because he is handsome? Is it because she has nice curves, or is it because of his nice arms? There is nothing wrong with being attracted to someone because of his or her physical qualities. It's a natural thing. But love goes deeper than that. It goes beyond the physical. It is about what is inside each individual. It is about the deep connection that you have with that person. It is about whether you're in tune with each other. When looking for love, you have to go beyond the physical. Our physical appearances will not last forever. We all grow older and at some point, lose some of our original physical sparkle. But mentality, heart, and character last forever. When you love someone because of what is inside him or her that is what will last forever. If anything, those internal qualities will make you want to go the extra mile.

Love. It is not an easy thing to find. So when you do find it, cherish it, nurture it, and protect it. Don't give up on it so easily. Fight for that love. You do that, and everlasting love and happiness can be yours now and forever.

Letting Go

Letting go. Letting go of someone or something is not an easy thing to do. There comes a point when we need to let go. No matter how much we want to, holding onto it will do you more harm than good. What was meant to be was meant to be.

You met someone. The person had everything you could ever want in a partner. Things were going great. You were as happy as you could be. You were the *it* couple. You were the next power couple. Then the individual broke your heart. You mourned the loss of your relationship. As time passes, out of the blue your ex resurfaces, wanting to rekindle the flame. Tempting isn't it? As good as it was the first time, you need to move on. If it were meant to last, you would still be together. Remember how you felt the first time things ended. Remember he or she was the one who screwed it up. Look at what you have going for you. Do you really want someone who didn't appreciate you before to come and screw everything up? That ship has sailed. It's time to let the person go.

Once upon a time, you were the best in the world in your position. You served that role with distinction. You were the world heavyweight champion. You were unstoppable. You went out on your terms as a champion. You left a lasting legacy in your sport. You achieved everything you set out to achieve and maximized your potential. Now you want to attempt a comeback after ten years away. Why? What do you have to prove? And more importantly, what do you have to gain? Things are different now. Think about your family. You have a beautiful family who loves and adores you. Think about all your other interests. Even if you were to return after all this time, would you be at the same level? Or are you just setting yourself up for disappointment? You have everything to lose and nothing to gain, so why do you need to do this? Time catches up to even the greatest of us. You had your time and proved you were the best. Now sit back, relax, and enjoy the fruit of your labours. It's time to let it go.

It's not always people we have trouble letting go of. Sometimes places are hard to let go as well. Take university for instance. I'm sure we all remember our time at university. The lectures, the all-night studying, the nights out. All those trips we were able to go on. The facilities that you get in university are in some cases second to none. Maybe we should go back one last time. Or should you? It is never the same the second time round. The people you were with then are no longer there. Things have changed. Perhaps your old halls of residence has been knocked down and replaced. Nothing is ever the same when you go back. Cherish the memories you had at university, but it's time to let go.

It's time to let go. What is done is done. Let bygones be bygones. It's time to move on. Now let it go.

I Am

I am here. I will always be here. I will always look after you. I will do everything in my power to look after you. I am everything you want me to be and then some.

I am your light, your guardian angel. I am the one who watches over you. I will follow you like a shadow. I am going to be there for you always.

I am always looking for ways to better myself. I am always looking to become the best version of myself. I am not perfect; I make mistakes. I am only human after all. But I will never stop trying to be perfect.

I am going to pay back the faith you have shown in me. You have given me support when no one else would. You believed in me when all seemed lost. I am going to do everything I can not to let you down.

I am the one. Your search is over. You don't need to look anymore. I am the one who is going to make you happy. I am the one who is going to stick with you through thick and thin. Whatever you need, I will do the best to provide it. I am not going away. I am going to be right here by your side.

I am going to do everything I can to make this work. I am going to do everything I can to make you happy. All I need is your trust, love, and support, and we can do anything we want.

You're the One I Want

I've searched my entire lifetime to meet someone special. The one with whom I can gladly spend the rest of my days. Alas, my search is over. I've found you, and you found me. You're the one I want. You're all I need. I simply want to be with you and don't want anybody else.

I want to be your blanket; I want to be the one you turn to when you get cold. I want to be the one who provides you with shelter when you feel alone. I want to be the one who feeds you when you're hungry. You're the one I want.

During my darkest moments, you were there. When I was worried and not sure where my next penny was coming from, you stood by my side. Whenever I felt like giving up, you gave me the will to fight on and never give up. You're the spark that illuminates me. You're the one I want.

Whenever I'm sad, hurt, or upset, just thinking of you is enough to turn that frown upside down. You're my guide whenever I get lost. You're the one who puts a spring in my step. There is no one I would rather have in my corner than you when the chips are down. I love you. You're the one I want.

Missing You

I miss you. You may have only gone away for a few days,
but it feels like you've been gone for months.
When you're not around, there is a big void in my heart.
I feel like I'm missing my other glove.

I'm missing you.
When you're around, I feel like there is sunshine every day.
When you're around, I feel complete.
I miss your comfort, your warmth, and most of all, I miss your love.

I'm missing you.
I miss the way you encourage me.
I miss the way you smile. But most of all, I miss you.
Your sheer presence fills me with joy.
I can't wait till you're back.
The end of your trip can't come soon enough.

I'm missing you.

WAR

The Man Who Went to War and Won

It would become the greatest battle any man could face. A battle that would last a lifetime. But it is a battle well worth fighting for.

And so it begins the battle to end all battles. The war to end all wars. The greatest challenge known to humanity. Ready or not, the war has just begun.

As a man steps onto the battlefield for maybe the first and last time, the fight begins. One man fighting the war—a war of desperation, a war without an end in sight. All alone without an ally in reach. He wonders what difference he can make. He asks if he is wasting his time, or if he can truly do something. The answer is yes he can. He can do a lot. One man can make a difference. In fact, one man can be the difference. In fact, he is the difference. A single man he may be, but he won't be alone. He'll have his wits, body, and will. The key to his success will be what's inside him, his inner spirit.

The inner spirit. A man's inner pride. It's the burning desire and hunger that all warriors need. The ability to rise to the challenge and boldly go where no one has gone before. A warrior's pride is a man's greatest weapon.

The war itself. War is being fought everywhere. Even as we speak, war is breaking out all over the world. The earth is in a state of constant battle. The question is when the time comes for him to enter the battle, when the time comes for him to stand up and be counted, will he be ready?

Ready he shall be. Like a duck to water, his very existence is defined by the war he faces each and every day. No matter how huge the obstacle, no matter how impossible the task maybe, he will be ready.

War has its up and downs. The scars, the hurt, the anger, the memories—war has it all. Battles are fought and won in many places and on many levels. Some wars are within; other wars are against people.

Whatever the war is, it is one he is prepared to win. No matter what the cost, he is prepared to carry on fighting. No matter where the battle takes him, no matter what the danger he was and will be in, he will continue the fight like a true warrior.

War. A man once said all it takes is one bad day to lose everything. With war, a second is all it takes. As is the case with this man. Just one bad piece of luck, one wrong turn, and the tide starts to turn against him. He starts to lose the war. He's losing pretty badly. He has nowhere to run, nowhere to hide. It's as if the whole world has turned against him, forcing him into a small corner. He's tired and weak. He can barely stand. What does he do?

He remembers his mission. He remembers why he started fighting. He remembers his quest, his dream, his goal, and his destiny. He remembers his family. But mostly, he remembers who he is. He gets up, licks his bruises, and readies himself for battle once again. As Napoleon once said, "A strong mind can overcome a fragile body." The war is not over, and he has a job to do. There's a battle going on, and he's ready to resume the fight.

The odds are against him. He's outnumbered, outmanned, outgunned. The one thing to remember about a war is you can never ever be truly certain of the outcome. If he plays his cards correctly, he can still win the game. Never lose hope, and never surrender. He has a chance. Skill and strategy can always beat even the most invincible of opponents.

The resumption of the war. It's now him vs. the world. To fight a war, he must become war itself. The problem he has is that he is still just a man. He's just pure flesh and blood. Tough! Use it. Turn every weakness into a strength. If he's going to go down, he'll give them hell before he does. The time has come for him to unleash the warrior inside. His time has come. He must finish what he has started. Now is the time for him to go out and win this war. He may be a man, but men, when they set their minds to it, can achieve anything. He makes himself more than a man. He devotes himself to an ideal, and if they can't stop him, not only will he win the war, he'll become something else entirely: a legend! Now the war is truly on. There's just one thing left to say, three words in fact. Just bring it!

As the war reaches its climax, the end is in sight. Just one final battle, one final hurdle, and then its all over. They already think it's all over, and it is now. Or is it?

The end of the war has come. All the endless fighting, inner turmoil, and struggle are finally over. The pain ceases. But one must ask, "What now? Where does he go from here?" Now there is no challenge. No battles to be fought, no dreams to be fulfilled. The fighting can stop. The problem is it isn't that simple. Enough is never enough. After one challenge is overcome, he seeks his next challenge, or the next challenge finds him. Could it be that he secretly craves war? Could it be there exists a part of him that craves the fight? Could it be that he craves the excitement and the intensity war brings? Could it be that life itself is about keeping up the fight? Could it be that life itself is war consisting of never-ending battles? Like the saying goes, there's always one more battle to be won.

The war is never truly over. There is always one more battle to be fought. As long as man has courage, as long as he has the heart and the will, as long as there exists a single breath inside him, the war must go on. There's still work to be done. It is the quest, the dream, the game, the greatest challenge a man can ever overcome.

Did the man win the war? Yes, he did. It's just that he has to do it again and again and again and again ... I think you get the picture.

The Champion Within

A champion—something we all aspire to be. To be the best, to be the one, to be the king, to be the one who said, "I did it." To be the one who made it happen. Many of us say we want to be a champion. But how many of us asks, "What does it mean to be a champion?"

Ability yes, but we all know people with ability that have never made it. Hunger absolutely, bottle definitely. But being a champion isn't just about having certain qualities or having key ingredients. It's not something you can just place in a bottle; it's something deeper. It's something more. Being a champion is about looking at what is inside you. It's about the champion within.

The best champions are the ones who are able to look inside themselves, and when it really matters, know how to deliver. They are the ones who rise to the big occasion, the ones who, when the going gets tough, they can get rough. The ones you know will have your back and will run through walls all day long.

When I think of great champions, I think of people like Michael Johnson, Usain Bolt, Roy Keane, Pete Sampras, Boris Becker, Sir Alex Ferguson, Mohammed Ali, Nelson Mandela, Martin Luther King, Bill Gates, Steve Jobs, Allyson Felix, Serena Williams. Different arenas, different domains, and different characters, but what is the commonality? They all had a sense of purpose; they all knew what they wanted to do and went all out to do it.

Champions don't always win. In fact, sometimes they lose, often even, but that's when they rise to the challenge. It's easy to look good when you're on a roll, but it takes character to come back from a defeat and rise again and again. As the saying goes, it isn't about how hard you can get hit, it's about how many times you can get hit and pick yourself up.

Champions can rise in any area of life. Sometimes all you have to do is look at their eyes; look deep at what is inside them and what drives them. To be a champion will take a lot of effort, time, and dedication. But when you look inside of yourself, you will discover the force within— your chi, the eye of the tiger, or whatever you want to call it. And when you find that power inside yourself, you can become truly unstoppable.

No Surrender

You're giving up. You're calling it quits. You're offering to surrender. Sorry, but I don't buy it. You do not have permission to surrender, soldier. This isn't over.

All right, I admit the situation looks bad. You're down to your last dime. You feel tired and sore. You're out of breath. You've tried all sorts of avenues to make it work. You feel you've done everything you can. Or have you?

Ever heard of second wind? Don't lose hope. Where there is a will, there is a way. There is more than one way to skin a cat. It's time for a new plan. Maybe you need backup; maybe you need to try a new tactic. It isn't over till the fat lady sings. The final whistle hasn't been blown yet. The final round is still upon us. You're still in this tournament. You made the last round. You can still have a shot at glory.

You came all this way, and you want to bow out now. I don't think so. So dust yourself off, and pick up your sword. There is still a battle to be fought. Now on your feet soldier. You have a job to do.

To Be the Best

So you want to be the best. You want to be the number 1. You want to be on top. You have to ask yourself one question: How badly do you want it? What are you willing to sacrifice to be the best?

Are you willingly to sacrifice those nights out on a Friday? Are you willing to stay longer at work to get that key presentation, right? Are you willing to go that extra mile in training? Are you willing to study beyond the bare minimum to pass your course? Are you ready to be a student of your craft? To be the best, there is a lot of hard work, dedication, and sleepless nights ahead of you.

Being the best isn't just about the title. The title is just the cherry on top. The journey to the title is just as important. And on that note, don't take any shortcuts. Do it the right way or not at all. You only have to look at individuals like Ben Johnson and Marion Jones to see how their lives changed for the worse when they took the easy route. And play the game the right way. Don't just park the bus or be negative. There will be times when you need to dig deep and get stuck in, but a cowardly approach will not bring the rewards or fulfilment you seek. Know when to take a risk; understand what the right risks are. Being the best is also about making the right decisions at the right time.

To be the best, you will have to beat the best. If you want to be considered the best, you're going to have to step up to the big players eventually. No one will consider you the champion if you duck all the main contenders. You have to face them head-on if you really want to be respected. And to that end, when you become number 1, you have to train like you're the number 2. Never set yourself a glass ceiling.

The other thing you need to consider is why do you want it? What is it that is driving your obsession? Is it fame? Is it money? Money and fame are not good drivers. They can come when you're successful, but we all know stories of individuals with all the fame and money in the world yet are still very unhappy. Money and fame come and go, but glory lives forever. So if not fame and money, what then? What should we use to drive us on? Simple, it is your passion. Yes, passion.

To be the best, you need to have passion. You need to love what you do. You need to be obsessed with it. When you do that, you will naturally go the extra mile; you will naturally find that second wind. You will naturally seek to do it the right way. Go at it with the right desire and attitude, and eventually the results will come. Bit by bit, you will improve. And maybe, hopefully with some luck, you will get to your goal and become the best at whatever you want to be.

Now get up on your feet, soldier. What you waiting for? You have work to do.

The Power of the Mind

"The pen is mightier than the sword," they say, but to wield a pen, there needs to be a mind. A pen can be effective in the hands of a person with the right mindset. This is why a great mind can be a great weapon. To win a war, you need soldiers. Your soldiers may make up your army, but you still need a general to strategize and plot your way to victory.

The human body is a machine. Food and water are its power source. They are the fuel; they are what turn the engine on. But it is the brain that operates the body. It is the brain that tells it how and when to walk, how to run; when to slow down, and when to speed up. Your arms and legs may do the heavy lifting, but it is your mind's will that sees you through the task at hand. Your hands are maybe what are behind the wheel, but it is your brain that reacts to what it sees on the road. When training, don't train with your muscles; train with your mind. The right mindset can give you the mental toughness you need to make it through the hardest of tasks.

Not all opponents can be beaten through physicality alone. Sometimes you need to take a different route. Sometimes you need to out-think them. Wit and cunning are equally as important. Play your cards right; and the game can still be won. For instance, if you're up against a giant, bring him or her down to size and then attack. Plan A may not always be enough; create a Plan B, a contingency plan if you will, so that you're not caught off guard. Also, everyone can prepare for the expected. If your opponent is expecting one thing, why not do the opposite? Use your head, and keep your opponent guessing. Instead of the pen being mightier the sword, make your mind sharper than the person wielding the sword.

Never underestimate the power of the mind. Training is one thing, but the will to act and to have clean thoughts in the heat of battle can make the difference between winning and losing.

Respect

Respect. We all want to be respected, but do we respect ourselves?
Why is it you respect one person but not another person?
Have you unfairly discriminated against someone?
What does someone need to do to earn your respect?

The real question should be what you have done to ensure that the other people respects you.
Like trust, respect needs to be earned.
It can also be lost in an instant, so don't abuse it.
Respect and treat others in the way you want to be respected and treated.

Listen and understand before you judge someone.
Think about how your actions influence the way you get respect.
All of that make sense to you? Cool.
Respect.

Being the Difference

That was close. There was nothing to separate them. It really was too close to call. But in every contest, there has to be a winner. How do you separate two evenly matched opponents? Your guess is as good as mine. What was the difference between the two? It really was a case of winning by the slimmest of margins.

It can be a moment of magic. Sometimes it can be a mistake. Sometimes it can be seeing an opening when all other avenues appear lost. Sometimes you need to take a gamble. Maybe you just need one player to complete your line-up. We are always in search of that special ingredient. That extra topping to give us that little bit of sparkle. It doesn't take much to be the difference.

Sometimes you do need luck. But persistent winners cannot be lucky. It isn't luck when everything is on the line and they find a way to prevail. It isn't luck when they score so many last-minute winners. It isn't luck that they are always on the team-of-the-year awards. It isn't luck they are the ones that are always amongst the top-five exam scores. It isn't luck that year after year that they continue to deliver. The trophies are testaments to their abilities and consistency, but more importantly it is their willingness to stand up and be counted when needed. When it came down to it, the difference was mentality. It is what they have up there — the space between the ears — that sets them apart. Their mental states make the difference.

After so many times of trying, I couldn't get it. I always failed at the same turn. I always ended up not having enough time to finish all the questions. I always felt like I could do better. Now enough is enough. I am not accepting this any longer. I am not settling for second-best ever again. I'm going to do everything in my power to succeed. And guess what? Since I made that statement, I have never finished second again. Now I can do that right turn. Now I always have adequate time to finish my exams. I can't believe it. Just like that, everything has fallen into place. What changed? What made the difference? Simple—it was you.

Sometimes to be the difference you must take a deep look at yourself and ask yourself the difficult questions. Are you doing everything you can to succeed? Make sure you leave no stone untouched. Don't rule out anything. That extra five percent may be all you need to get over the finish line. Sometimes finding the final piece of the jigsaw puzzle is the toughest part of the challenge. Finding the final sticker to complete the album is always the tricky part. Sometimes you must look in places you didn't think you would ever consider. Maybe you need to try something that is very unfamiliar to you. Life takes us on all sorts of paths. There is more than one way to skin a cat after all.

With every door there is a key. No matter how many keys you may have on you, only one will open the door in front of you. When you find it, keep hold of it. Remember where you placed it; never lose it. Make sure it is there when you really need it. Keep a close eye on it. Once you know where it is, it will be there, waiting for you, when you need it most. Now you have everything you need to move forward. Now it is time to go and make a difference.

Why Are You Afraid?

Fear. Fear is one of the most dangerous emotions out there. Fear gets to the best of us. Fear can be a powerful instrument. It is used to control us, it is used to hurt us, and it is used to weaken us. Fear is everywhere. Fear can come out of nowhere. Fear can be there before the gun goes off. Fear can be there when you're about to sit your final exam. Fear can be there when you're going for a job interview. It is natural to be afraid.

So how do we overcome fear? There is no magic answer. Fear can be managed and overcome in many ways. There is a saying that to overcome fear, you must become fear. How do you become what you fear? Perhaps the answer lies in facing what you fear. What is it that you fear? In other words, what are you afraid of?

Fear often comes about because we keep asking ourselves what will happen if we fail? We often fear the consequences. What happens if we don't make it? Perhaps we should ask the opposite. What will happen if I get the job? What other opportunities will I get if I pass this exam? Where could this relationship go if I make it work? Instead of concentrating on what could go wrong, concentrate on what could go right. When you focus on the positive instead of the negative, half the battle is won. It's time to let go of your fear. So take a deep breath, relax, and give it your best shot. Are you ready? Good. Now on your marks, get set … go!

Being Inspired

Inspiration. What is inspiration? One definition is the process of being mentally stimulated to do or feel something. So we know what inspiration is, but how do we find it? The real question is, what inspires you?

Inspiration isn't some scientific formula. It isn't a question of what is right and wrong. It's about finding that spark. It's about identifying that trigger. It's about what fires you up. It's about what makes you get up in the morning. It's about finding the desire to get through even the hardest of workouts. It's about what makes you determined to get it done and finish the course. Inspiration is about dragging yourself over the line when you feel you are on your last breath. To be inspired is about looking deep inside yourself and bringing out something you didn't know you had.

Sometimes inspiration can come from the weirdest of places. My best ideas sometimes come after a hard session in the gym or on the track. Very often I go home or back to my desk and implement an idea I thought of literally seconds before. An idea could come to you when you're eating. Maybe it comes whilst you watch something on television. It may even come when you're sitting on the toilet. Sometimes it requires you to take a step back, take a deep breath, and let the inspiration come to you.

The other place we can find inspiration is in people. Maybe your childhood heroes inspire you. Maybe you remember their greatest sporting achievements or their great speeches. Maybe it's when they showed courage in the face of danger. Whomever you get inspiration from, the question to ask is; what was it about them that inspired you? What qualities do they possess and how can you obtain those same qualities?

Another place of inspiration can be found closer to home. We all forget to look there over and over again. Do you want to know what the answer is? It is staring you in the face. It's you. Yes, you. Think about it. Think back to all the tough situations you have been in over the years and what it took to overcome them. Think back to all the times you felt under pressure but managed to deliver. What was the driving force behind it? What was the motivation? It was you. Think back to when you set a personal best at something and all the hours it took to master your craft. Think about the most difficult exams you had to sit through. It was you at the heart of it. You can look to people who inspire you and those you admire, but no one can sit the exam for you. Perhaps you just needed someone to give you a pep talk. But sooner or later, you're going to have to be the one to walk through the door. Instead of looking for inspiration, try to be the inspiration. When you do that in your times of need, you will never have to look too far to become inspired.

Into the Shadows

Despair, darkness, suffering. A once-prosperous city is now struggling. Crime is rife; the police are overwhelmed. Hooligans and thugs now run this city. Even the kids are embroiled in this. Trouble is just around the corner in this city. We need help; someone who can turn the tide in our favour; someone who can rattle the cages. Will anyone answer this cry for help?

I still remember the day like it was yesterday when the call was answered. It was a cold night in February, and I was heading home after a long day at work. A gang of five suddenly made their way towards me. A minute later, I was surrounded. Outnumbered and outgunned, I thought this could be the end for me. And then all of a sudden, a whoosh was heard. All of a sudden, four of the gang members were left standing. "What just happened?" one of them asked. They all look puzzled.

Then thirty seconds later, another whoosh was heard. Two down, three to go. "Show yourself," one of them said.

Another one looked up into the sky and said, "Guys." We all looked up.

And there he was. A mysterious figure dressed in a black ninja battle suit, a mask concealing his face. In a matter of moments, I was the only one left standing. This man was a warrior; they couldn't get close to him. He had some of the fastest reflexes I had ever seen. It was as if I was seeing a modern-day Bruce Lee, Chuck Norris, Jean-Claude Van Damme rolled up into one. I was scared, shaken. I thought, *it's my turn next.*

I then heard a whisper. The whisper said, "Relax, I'm here to help. You can go home now. You're safe." I turned round, and all I saw was a fleeting shadow disappear into the background. Out of the shadows he came, and into the shadows he went.

I went home thankful for what had transpired. I thought I would never see or hear from this mysterious figure again. I was sure it was a one-off; I was lucky and received a guardian angel for the night. How wrong I was.

All of a sudden, I heard more stories of people being rescued when all seemed lost. The story was always the same. Out of the shadows he comes, and into the shadows he goes.

In an instant, hope returned to a broken city. The gloom and doom that spread over the city like a disease was slowly starting to evaporate. People started believing again. And now, evil had a new face to fear. The media went crazy over him. A mysterious warrior, a guardian angel. A protector they branded him. They dubbed him the "Shadow Master," the man who comes out from the shadows only to disappear back into the shadows.

A revolution had begun. A light was lit. People started to rise and stand up for what they believed in. For too long we were left to suffer in silence. The police were overrun and either too scared or frightened to protect us. Now we could fight together as a community, take back our once-proud city, and drive away this evil. All of this started due to the man who came from the shadows.

Things have been better than they have been for a long time. There was just one problem. When you challenge the established order, there are consequences. The Shadow Master had disturbed the so-called natural order. The money train had been halted as it were. When money talks, people listen. The Shadow Master, until now, had been the predator; now he was the prey, the one being hunted. A bounty was placed on him. Things were about to get ugly.

Numerous gangs and hooligans went searching for the Shadow Master. They tried to get information from the weak and innocent on where the Shadow Master may be. I was worried; I thought, *What will the Shadow Master do? He's just one man.* Little did I know that he expected all of this. He had a plan to take them all down.

One night a signal appeared in the sky for everyone to see. The signal said, "If you want me, midnight at the pier docks. Be there or else."

I thought, *is he mad? Him against the worst scum in the city? He won't survive this.* I grabbed my coat and picked up a baseball bat.

I went to the pier and waited behind some trees so I could stay out of sight. I stayed there and waited. Midnight came, and all the gangs arrived. I counted at least a hundred men. The leader of the bunch—the Big Bad as he's referred to in the media— screamed out, "Where are you?"

There was a sudden whoosh, and all I heard was a sharp whisper that said, "Here." The Shadow Master was there.

The battle began, one man against an army. Little did I know the Shadow Master had set some traps to slow down the army. At one point, he had the upper hand. He reigned down blow after blow after blow. They struggled to deal with his fury. I thought he may actually prevail. Then disaster occurred. Eventually, the army overwhelmed him, and he was beaten to a bloody pulp. Could this be the end of our saviour? The Big Bad, a gun in his hand, walked up to him. I thought, *No, this can't happen, not like this.*

The Big Bad asked the Shadow Master, "Any last requests?"

The Shadow Master replied, "Gotcha."

At that moment, I shouted no and stood up to face them. "If you want to take him down, you have to take me as well."

Another voice then screamed, "Me too!" More and more people suddenly emerged from the shadows to stand up for their hero. The scum found themselves outnumbered. The Shadow Master had helped many of us since he came onto the scene, and it was now our turn to help him. Now the Shadow Master had his army.

The Shadow Master knocked the gun out of the Big Bad's hand, and the fighting resumed. This time, the gangs of the city fell; many retreated. The Big Bad was taken down by the Shadow Master. We chained him up and celebrated. Finally, the evil that had taken over the city was cleaned up.

We then heard sirens. The police were on their way, finally showing a backbone once all the hard work had been done for them. I turned round and I could see that the Shadow Master was about to do his disappearing act. I said, "Wait. You came here alone to face many. How did you know we would come to help you?"

He smiled and said, "Simple. It was hope." A flash of smoke appeared, and he was gone. Back into the shadows from which he came.

Since that night, the city has become a beacon of hope. Crime has ceased. Kids are free to go out and play. I can rest easy at night. The Shadow Master hasn't been seen or heard from since. His work was done.

I now see his real mission. It wasn't to be a one-man army. It wasn't to be a saviour. It was to bring hope and to unite the people to save themselves. Maybe someday, if and when we need him, we will see him again. Until then, in the shadows he will remain.

Never-Ending

Today, yesterday, and tomorrow. It never ends. The continuous battle, the continuous fight, the continuous war. All this struggle and for what? Sometimes I wonder why I fight. What do I need to prove? What is it that I seek? Does the end justify the means; is the struggle worth it? Could it be that our survival depends on it?

When do we stop— when our luck runs out? When we can fight no more? Life is a battle; it's what we live for. We live it, breathe it, eat it, and even sleep it. But in those struggles, amongst all the hurt and anxiety, there is light at the end of the tunnel. A silver lining to a grey and dark cloud. There is a path of fire that can lead to the greatest rewards.

Only when we have the courage and heart to walk down that path will the end be in sight. When we reach into what's inside us. If you become more than just a number, if you believe in an ideal, you can win. Demand success and only success. When the time is right, the never-ending will cease to be. The never-ending will become the everlasting.

With Honour

Honour. To be honourable is about fighting with integrity. It's about doing the right thing, no matter the cost. It's about showing the upmost dignity. It is about respecting others the way you would respect yourself.

Honour is about fighting till the very end, even when all seems lost. Victory can be claimed from the jaws of defeat. You can come back from two sets to love down. It is not about giving up at the first sign of trouble. When in your heart you know something is right, real honour is following through on those convictions, not bowing down to peer pressure or general opinion. They may hate you at the beginning, but they will respect you for it in the end.

Sometimes you may end up having to stand alone. Sometimes the right path can be a lonely one. Being honourable is not a popularity contest. It's about acting with the best of intentions. And be careful about making promises you can't keep. Aim to do your best, and if you fall short, no one will say that you acted without honour.

Honour is about respecting people's memory. When someone is gone, all that is left are the memories of someone and their legacy. On occasion, you may even have to follow in their footsteps. When doing so, all you can do is make your own path. But remember their values, beliefs, and what they stood for. That is the best way to honour their memories.

Victory that isn't earned fairly is cheating. Victory you didn't deserve is not glorious. A victory that you know in your heart was not right is not the way to go. There is no honour. There is no shame in defeat, but there is no honour in not fighting at all.

Rage

Rage, outraged. I have never been so offended in my entire life. I'm really angry. I'm angry enough to go out there and really hurt someone. I'm angry enough to bang my head against the wall. I'm very cross about this situation. I'm so angry that I just want to take it out on the first person or persons that I see. And guess what I go out and do. I proceed to do exactly that. And then the penny dropped.

What did I just do? I just went out and really hurt someone. I just said something I regret to someone. The person in question may have offended me in the first place, gotten on my nerves, been the one to wrong me in the first place, or simply been in the wrong place at the wrong time. But the person did not deserve that. Two wrongs do not make a right. That's the problem with rage. It causes you to do things you wouldn't do when you are thinking normally.

Rage — to be so angry that you're out of control is not a good place to be. It's a path that leads to darkness, pain, and suffering. And do you know who you're hurting the most? It's you. Being angry is a natural thing. Sometimes people know how to push your buttons. But don't let it affect your focus. Don't let it make you do something you're only going to regret.

Rage can bring out a side of you that you didn't know existed. Sometimes you don't know what you can do when you're angry. Sometimes you don't know your own strength. Letting rage get the better of you is a no-win situation. So what do we do to control rage? Do we bottle it up inside? No, rage is like a beast. When you cage the beast, it gets angry. And when the beast gets lose, it often results in a fury unlike any other that's ever been unleashed. No, we're not going to bottle it up; we're going to use it. But we're going to use it constructively.

Rage can bring about several things. Uncontrollable rage is useless.

However intensity, focus, and the will to right a wrong are weapons. Bring those with you. If you like going to the gym, take your focus there, and give yourself a pounding session. Your body will thank you for it later. Perhaps you enjoy running. If that's the case, go for a run; run like there is no tomorrow. Perhaps you're creative; maybe you're an artist or like to bake. Go away and turn that rage into focus and desire to make your best painting or cake ever. Before you know it, you have created your masterpiece.

Perhaps you prefer a more calming influence, so maybe try something simple. Whatever you do, make sure you channel that rage into something positive. After all is said and done, take a step back, take a deep breath, and relax. Feel better? Good. Remember that the next time you feel that rage is starting to consume you.

Anger may prepare you for the battle, but it is a lousy weapon. So the next time someone does something to anger you and you find yourself in a serious state of rage, don't get mad. Get even.

Go for It

Well this is it. The moment you've been waiting for.
You've trained all your life for this.
This is everything you have been working towards.
It's time to finish the job. Go for it.

Are you scared? Are you nervous? Don't be.
You've done everything possible to make this be successful.
Now it's all about trusting your instincts and remembering everything
you've been taught.
So go for it.

You've come so far. This is the final hurdle. This is the last lap.
I know you're tired. Never end your session on a downer.
Always end it on a high.
So come on now, one last big effort.

Just one more lap, and then it is all over.
A cold shower and good food awaits you.
So what are you waiting for?
Just go for it.

Beating the Unstoppable

Unstoppable: the irresistible force, the unmovable, the unbeatable, the undeniable. A foe that has never ever been beaten. A foe that is larger than life. An opponent that is unconquerable. It's very presence brings fear to even the bravest. Have you ever witnessed anything like this? So that just leaves one question: How do you beat the unstoppable?

So where do you begin. How about sizing up your opponent? Opponents can come in all shapes and forms. For instance, if you're up against a giant, take them down to size and then attack. The opponent may have more physical strength then you; maybe you can get stronger or use your speed or wits. Can your opponent out-think you? What if your opponent is not human? Your opponent may not be physical. Maybe you can try the eyes-closed technique. Use your imagination. Imagine the perfect execution of bringing down your opponent. Think happy thoughts; think triumphant thoughts.

There is one other obstacle to face when facing the unstoppable. What is that obstacle? Do you really want to know? Well, simply look in the mirror. The other obstacle to overcome is you. Yes, you. Think about it. Think back to some of the hardest things you've ever had to overcome. What was your real biggest opponent? What held you back? Was it your fear? Was it your preparation or training? Did you get enough sleep? To face the unstoppable, you must make sure you're ready. If you have doubts or are not physically or mentally ready, you've already lost. To face the unbeatable is not just about beating the unstoppable; it's also about you. In fact, it starts with you.

The final thing to remember is no one is ever unbeatable. The trick is to make yourself as tough to beat as possible. Set the bar so high that it will take a ridiculous amount of effort to beat you. You may end up falling just short. We are only human after all. If you don't get the desired outcome but can look at yourself and say you did your absolute best and left no stone unturned, you've won. Only when you are at this point will the unstoppable become not so unstoppable anymore.

Making the Impossible Possible

In my lifetime, I have seen many things I never thought I would see. I have seen a British player win Wimbledon. I have seen my beloved Manchester United win the treble. I have seen players score from the halfway line. I've seen the first black US president. I've seen the Avengers come to life. Michael Johnson's 200 and 400 meter world records have been broken; I honestly thought those records would be around for the rest of my lifetime. I have seen a home Olympics and been to the Commonwealth Games. All these were things at one point that seemed impossible.

We as a species have come very far. Whoever thought we would ever see man land on the moon? Whoever thought we would have a device that allows us to talk to anyone in the world whenever we want? Go back a hundred years, to when travelling from continent to continent took days, weeks, and sometimes months. Now I can hop on a plane and be there in a few hours. All these things seemed nigh on impossible not long ago.

It's amazing what we can do when we put our minds to it. I used to wonder what it would take to bench press 100kg. I used to wonder what it would be like to own a car and drive. I used to think about becoming a homeowner. Now I can bench press 125kg and counting. I have a car and am a homeowner. Years ago, those things seemed impossible. Yet step by step, I got closer to those goals, and now the dreams are reality.

The thing to remember is that nothing is impossible. Mountains can be climbed. Where there is a will, there is a way. The trick is to have a plan and break down the steps required to get to your success. To boldly go where you haven't gone before may require a leap of faith. It may involve going to places you didn't envisage. But look at all the great inventions that we have today—electricity, light, the internet. They were all ideas and concepts that were turned into reality. All these ideas were at one point impossible. The impossible becomes possible when we start trying and believing. It is when we don't give in that things can happen.

No one knows what the future holds. No one can predict what is going to happen in twenty years. The only thing we can do is to live our lives the best we can. We have to keep on pushing the barriers and discovering new ways of doing things. As long as we keep on doing that, what maybe science fiction today will become reality. Only then will the impossible become the possible.

Glory

Glorious

Glorious; it was a glorious day. Everyone was absolutely right. Everything was spot on. It was sensational. It was fantastic. It was absolutely glorious, a moment that I will remember forever and forever.

I never thought I would experience anything like this. Today we will celebrate like there is no tomorrow. Let us rejoice. It was everything I expected. It was amazing. It was sweet. It was just glorious.

There are some moments in life that simply take your breath away, and today was one of those days. I have been waiting for a performance like that. It was the day when everything clicked. It was a day when all the pieces fell into place. It was the perfect moment. It was an outstanding accomplishment. It was simply glorious.

But this glory isn't just about me. It is a glory I want to share with my friends and family. Without them, none of this would have been possible. I want them to cherish this moment alongside me. I want them to be also glorious.

Remember this day; remember this moment. This will be with you forever. Enjoy it as it was just simply glorious.

The Greatest Ever

The greatest I have ever seen. This person was magnificent. He could do things with a football that I could only dream of. He made the impossible look possible. The goals he scored, the matches he won, the teams he played for—absolutely amazing.

Just what was it that made him so good? The great goals. The great matches. Those breathtaking moments which made me wonder, *did he really just do that?* And he didn't just do it against the small teams; he did it in the big matches. He did it against the best of the best of the best. Season in, season out, his level of commitment never wavered. Rain, snow, or wind, when the whistle blew, it was go time.

The way he dribbled was as if the ball was stuck to his feet. Anyone would have thought he had a ball magnet inside his boots. And when he moved, he didn't just simply run; he glided across the pitch. It was like watching a ballerina. It really was poetry in motion. He was the general; he was the engine. He was the one who kept the team ticking over.

I still remember that dribble from the halfway line. He took out the entire team before rifling it into the top corner from twenty-five yards. I still remember the way he always demanded the ball, no matter how many defenders were on him. He was always the player the opposition feared. He was the one who could make the difference. At times, it was simply a case of give him the ball, and he would figure out what to do with it.

I was honoured to be around whilst this guy was playing. Here's to you, sir. I think I speak for all your fans when I say, "Thanks for all the memories."

Victory

Game, set, and match. The final whistle is blown. You've reached the end of the session. You've completed your final exam. You nailed that interview. Congratulations, you've done it. At last you've won. Well done. Victory is yours. A victory that seemed a long way off at one stage is now yours.

All the blood, sweat, and tears. This is what you trained for, this is what you fought for, and this is what you studied for. Moments like these are what make life worth living. The sweet taste of victory; it's the light at the end of the tunnel. It truly was sensational. Who would have thought we would have ran out 5–3 winners, especially being 3–0 down at halftime. Who would have thought you would be winning the grand slam when you were two sets down? Victory is in sight' let's not blow it now. It isn't over until it is over.

How did you achieve this victory? Luck? You made your own luck. Victory was not some divine outcome. Coaching? Coaches can only show you the door. A coach can show you the path, but you still have to walk the path yourself. They can't get the victory for you. Skill? Probably. Desire and hunger absolutely. But don't forget the thing that lies deep inside you. It's belief. Despite how far off it seemed, despite how desperate things may have gotten, you didn't give in. You didn't surrender, and now you have your reward. If you did not believe in yourself, that victory would not have been possible. Faith in yourself was the key to this great victory.

Savour this victory. When you're down and out, think back to this day. Think back to this situation, a situation where you couldn't see a way out, a situation in which you thought victory was impossible. Remember this day always. Remember the day of your greatest triumph, your greatest victory. Remember what it took to get that win. Remember how deep inside of yourself you had to reach. Remember the strength and courage you had to muster to secure that victory. You've done it before, and you can do it again.

Behind every victory is a story. The path to victory is very often not easy. But victory is just one part of the story. The victory is the result. It's the path to the victory that makes it really victorious. That really was a sweet victory.

The King

The time has come. Our King is here; our Saviour, the one who will lead us to victory. The one who will lead us to glory. The one who will lead us into battle. Glory is around the corner. This is someone I can get behind and lend them my support.

He is the heir to the throne, the next in line, the next in a great legacy. He will continue our great traditions. He will take us to places where no king has ever gone before. The King is here. The one who represents us. The one who looks out for his people. A warrior, a king. His wisdom he shares with us freely; he takes time out to get to know his people.

A new dawn has arisen. A new era is about to begin. The King is here. Arise, the King has come. He is finally here. His time has come. The one who will deliver us to the Promised Land. The king is dead; long live the King.

Legacy

Life is something we only have one shot at, and it doesn't last very long. Someday we will no longer be here. With that in mind, what will be left behind long after we depart this world? Money, material belongings, loved ones. Those will definitely be left behind. But there is something else that we will leave behind—a legacy.

Long after we go, our names live on in memories. Our deeds will be remembered. Our actions will be scrutinized. The decisions we make will be felt by many for years to come. The things we leave our name on, the associations we make, the impact we have on people all contribute to our legacies. No matter what we do in life, the legacy of what we did remains.

How do you want to be remembered? What do you want to give back to the world once you're gone? Did you look after your family? Were you there for them in times of need? Maybe you had a talent for a particular sport. Did you make the most of your talent? Were you as humble in defeat as you were in victory? Did you leave your workplace in a better position than when you first arrived? Outside of work, what were you like to your fellow human beings. Did you treat others as you would like to be treated? Did you give as much as you took? All these things will make up your legacy.

A legacy is a lasting impression of how you are remembered. But that's the good thing. The legacy is something you can shape. It is something that you can control. You can define what legacy you want to leave for this world. You need to own it and act on it. You have it within you to shape the future. Once you do that, the world is your oyster. That's one of the beauties we have in life; we can shape it as we see fit. We all create our own legacies. Now go and create yours.

The Supreme Champion

Every so often, you meet a once-in-a-lifetime talent. A person so gifted he or she transcends all who have come before them. Some champions are made, and then there are those born champions. Never have I seen someone like this. This is a truly unique and exceptional person. This is a real special one. This person is the supreme champion.

I have seen many great superstars and champions in different walks of life. But what we have here is someone unique. Never have I witnessed someone who brings grace, power, balance, skill, and the ability to execute his game flawlessly. He is as cool as a cucumber under pressure. He has nerves of steel. He makes Bjorn Borg look like he's having a tantrum. Yet with that calm, he is able to exert such ruthless precision that no matter what obstacle is presented to him, he still gets the job done. He's overcome injury, new rivals, changing rules, and still manages to stay on top. Getting to the top is one thing, but it takes a truly exceptional effort to stay there. Yet after ten years and counting, he is as supreme as ever. A truly remarkable feat by a supreme champion.

There are so many victories and accomplishments to walk through. We can dedicate a highlights reel to this person and still be wanting more. He is the benchmark future champions will be measured against. He has redefined what it means to be a champion. Decades from now, we will still be talking about this individual. This person will be an inspiration to the world for many years to come. The best there is, the best there was, and most definitely, the best to have ever graced this planet. A worthy status and one that is befitting the supreme champion.

Is this really a person; is this person real? Can such a human being actually exist? It isn't just the titles or the victories that makes this person so special. It's the down-to-earth, gentle manner. A person who doesn't act better than everybody else; a person who goes out of the way to help everybody. There is a saying about nice guys finishing last. Well, this person clearly didn't read the memo. This individual tore up the rulebook about how champions are meant to be and created his own script, a script befitting the supreme champion.

This person has defeated all opponents and conquered all challenges. This person really is the phenomenal one, the champion of champions. This is really the supreme champion.

The Time Is Now

It is time. The time has come. It is time for you to arise and be all that you were meant to be. It is time for you to seize your opportunity. It's your time to shine. You've had to be patient; you've had to get in line and wait in what seemed like a never-ending queue. But now you are about to get everything you deserve. The time is now.

All those times you were told you had to wait, all those times people said you would not get the opportunity, all those times people said you weren't good enough, all those times people said it wasn't possible; well, look at you now. Now the light bulb is on, and everything has clicked. All the pieces have been assembled; everything is in place for you to succeed. You have the skill and knowledge. People have your back, and now the will is there. Now is your moment. Now it is your time. The time is now.

You remember all the people at school who used to laugh at you. Well, they're not laughing at you now. When they see you now, a lot of them comment on how good you look. And let's not forget all those people who used to turn you down when it came to dating. Now they're coming to you. It is time; the time is now. Enjoy it.

I remember a time when people used to moan at you. "Oh, why are you still living at home with your mum? How come you're not driving yet? When are you going to make vice president?" But look at you now. You knew what you were doing. Good for you for sticking to your plan. Your time is now; now you can celebrate.

Where there was once moaning, there is now praise. Where there was sacrifice, there is now reward. Where there was chaos, there is now peace. What people didn't realize was you had your plan, you had your path. People go on different journeys. Sometimes to get from A to B, you may have to encounter C, D, and E first. But now your journey is complete. The time is now. Go and enjoy your reward.

Everyone matures at different rates. Now you have the right opening, the right opportunity, the right person. It was just a matter of timing. The time is now. It's yours; take it. You've worked hard to get to this point. You have the ball; you have the seat. What you do with it is up to you.

A Day to Remember

This really is a day to remember. I'm going to remember this day for the rest of my life. It's the sort of day that everyone wishes for. Absolutely everything went right. From the moment I got out of bed this morning, I knew I was in for something special. The sun was out, and my neighbours were smiling. Why can't every day be like this?

I saw something I never thought I would see. I did something that I never thought I would ever do. What I have just seen was amazing. I'm lost for words at what I just saw. For me, this is right up there with man walking on the moon. It is a picture-perfect moment. It is a moment that I will replay in my mind over and over again.

To have such a day which not only had an impact on you but had a great impact on the people around you. In fact, the whole world was impacted by this. It's the sort of day that makes you think anything is possible. Believe the hype; it was a good as everything you've heard. It really was magical. You had to be there to really believe it.

Today truly was special. I will never forget this day. Today was one for the memories.

The Next Big Thing

Wow, what a behemoth. I have never seen anyone with the traps this guy has. He has the strength of a bull, he's as agile as a cat, and he can sting like a butterfly and float like a bee. It's almost as if he were Mohammed Ali the second. This guy is going to dominate the squared circle for years to come. He is the next big thing.

On your marks, get set, go. And he's done it again. That was an easy win in the end. The next dominant sprinter has landed, the favourite for the Olympic Games. He will be the next great sprint champion. Surely there is no stopping him. The question is not if he will win but what time he will win it in. Athletics has a new star. This guy is the next big thing.

This is it. This invention is going to change the world. This invention is going to change the way we do business. This is going to make us millions. This invention is going to be the next big thing.

Where did you get that jacket? It's very nice. I'm suddenly seeing this jacket all over the place? It's from the new fashion designer. Really, tell me more. It is so smooth and so silky. What is the jacket made of? Within the next few years, all jackets will be made of this material. It really is the next big thing.

Ten straight games won. Thirty-one goals scored and none conceded. Nine points clear already. I say surrender; the title race is done. They're playing with a style and swagger I have not seen since the days of the Manchester United teams of the Sir Alex Ferguson – era or the Arsenal Invincibles of 2004. Game, set, and match. I will love it if they do it. Love it. This team is the next big thing.

The next big thing, huh. Where have I heard that before? We are always looking for something new. Always ready to announce the new heir to throne. Sometimes before him, she, or whatever it is has truly proved themselves. Having potential is one thing; turning that potential into a reality is another.

We have all seen false dawns. Some people that we expect to do well don't do as well as expected. For every wonder kid that goes on to do well in a sport, others end up wasting their talents. I've seen teams blow twelve-point leads; comebacks can happen. You can come back from three goals down and win 5–3. It isn't over till the trophy is officially handed out.

Just because someone was exceptional at nineteen doesn't mean the person will be as exceptional at twenty-seven or twenty-eight. People and things mature at different times. Even if you do it now, how do you know you can come back and do it again next year? You have to prove you're not just a one-season wonder, a flash in the pan, or a fluke. So what needs to happen to ensure the next big thing becomes the big thing?

Unfortunately, nothing is guaranteed in life. There is no magic pill that you can take for such things. The one thing we can do is work on it. Whatever talent, opportunity, or idea you have, make sure to work on it. Give it your best shot. Don't waste the opportunity that you have ahead of you. Being predicted nine A's is not the same thing as receiving nine A's. It's about walking the walk.

Okay, so maybe you do have the gift. Maybe you do have a skill or strength that has never been seen before. Maybe you are really as good as they say you are. But until you get the title or titles, just know your role; be humble, put in the graft, and get to work. Then given time, if the conditions are right someday, hopefully instead of people referring to you or the gift you have as the next big thing, they will call you the big thing. I'll be waiting and smiling at you when this happens. The journey to the title is just as important as the title itself. Hopefully one day I will happily have the opportunity to refer to you as the big thing.

The Man with the Midas Touch

The man with the Midas touch. Everything he touches turns to gold. He is such a silky, smooth operator. I've never seen him break a sweat.

He is the man with the plan. He is the master planner. He is as tech savvy as they come. He is a real-world Tony Stark. His innovations make Q from *James Bond* appear to be a rank amateur. He really does have the Midas touch.

He is a cool as they come. I've never seen him buckle under pressure. He doesn't hide from anything. If anything, he lives for pressure. He thrives off it. It seems to bring out the best in him. Just when he appears to be at the boiling point, he goes out and hits a home run. He really does have the Midas touch.

So many business adventures he has undertaken. Every single one of them has been a success. He does not have a single black mark against him. He has gone into markets no one would ever think of touching and into places where no one would ever think of looking. He sees opportunities where everybody else only sees the threats. With this man, chaos equals opportunity. He really has the Midas touch.

Watching him up close is another story. Just observing the way he works, the way he weaves his magic, and the way he manages clients and his people, he makes all this interaction tick like clockwork. It really is an education on how to conduct business. The most amazing thing is he does all this with a smile. There is no crudeness, no arrogance. He's just a man who knows he has a God-given talent to go out there and make things happen. When the chips are down, you know he will last the distance. If you want someone who can get you out of a jam, this guy is your man. If you want a man who can turn a rough diamond into the finished article, he is the man. He really is the man with the Midas touch.

On Top of the World

Finally, you have done it. You've achieved your goal. You've climbed to the top of the mountain. You're sitting on top of the food chain. You really are on top of the world. And you earned it.

So how did all this come about? It came through hard work, focus, and dedication. All those sleepless nights and all the sacrifices you have made to get here have finally paid off. You're coming into a wonderful period in your life. Be grateful, be thankful, and be happy as you truly earned it.

It didn't come easy. The view is nice from the top, isn't it? You have the nice office next to the window and a personal assistant to manage your calendar. You get the star treatment. Now you are the VIP. Just remember it is a long way down, and the descent is often harder than the climb in the first place. It can also be lonely. Now you're at the top, you're the one to beat. The predator has become the prey. You're the one they're all looking up to. They're coming after you. Are you up to the challenge? Of course you are. You wouldn't have gotten your spot if you weren't. People believed in you and trust you in the position you now find yourself. Don't forget to believe in yourself.

Now you're at the top, you may end up encountering a lot of sharks. Wolves in sheep's clothing, so to speak. Be wary; stay alert, but don't be paranoid. And most importantly, be fair. Remember your manners, and don't betray your principles. Don't become an arrogant fool just because of your new status. At the end of the day, it is still just a title. You can shape the world as you see it. Just don't forget to bring others along with you, and don't be a jerk along the way.

Getting to the top is one thing. Staying there is another challenge. Train and work as if you're number 2. Keep on improving, and keep on learning. The moment you stop improving is the moment you stand still.

But more importantly, remember the people who helped you on your way to the top. Always remain humble, and don't ever forget who you really are. Keep your feet on the ground. Always be thankful, and look after those who have helped you along the way.

Enjoy your time at the top. Like life itself, nothing lasts forever. Time catches up to even the greatest of us. The end will come. It may be because of injury, maybe you get replaced, or maybe you have the opportunity to go out on your own terms ala Sir Alex Ferguson or Pete Sampras after his 2002 US Open win. Enjoy it whilst it lasts. You've earned your time in the spotlight. Now, go and be on top of the world.

Thank You

I just want to say one thing: thank you. Thank you for all that you have done for me. For every tear you wiped from my eye, for every time you bandaged my wounds, for every time you picked me up when I fell over, I just want to say thank you.

When I was thirsty, you gave me a glass of water. When I was hungry, you made sure there was food on the table. When I was cold, you provided me shelter. When I needed a ride home, you made sure I got home safely. For this I just say thank you.

I remember all the times that I was lonely, you provided me with companionship. When I was heartbroken, you provided me with love. When I needed to get something off my chest, you lent me your ears. When I needed your advice, your guidance really helped and directed me. For this I just want to say one thing, and that is thank you.

Some of the steps I have taken these past few years. You were with me every step of the way. I could not have done any of this without you. Thank you for being there when it really mattered.

When I first came into this role, I didn't believe I could do it. I thought I wasn't ready. But the moment you came into my life, you immediately saw something in me that I didn't see in myself. You gave me the platform to perform and excel, and helped grow my confidence. For this I say thank you.

In life, we sometimes need a helping hand. Sometimes we need a little pick-me-up. No matter how small or big the deed; never forget anyone who helped you when you needed it. But most of all, never forget to tell that person or persons one thing. And that is thank you.

Thanks for everything.

LIFE
STORIES

When Is Enough, Enough?

Enough. Aren't you full yet? Can your stomach really eat all that food? If you really are that hungry, then great. You really are a big eater. Just remember that others have to eat as well.

So you've bought another house. Well done, but did you really need that house? How big is your family? Do you really need ten bedrooms? Fifteen kitchens; is that really necessary? What are you planning to do? Do you intend to feed the five thousand? Some people don't even have a single roof over their heads, yet here you are, buying yourself another house. And you wonder why you ended up bankrupt.

Did you really need that last drink? The amount of trouble you have caused. You embarrassed yourself. How can you know that you enjoyed something if you can't even remember a single thing that happened? By all means, go out and enjoy yourself. Have fun, but know your limits.

Did you really need to say that? I mean seriously, look at the person. The person is crying. You're made the individual's life miserable. You really hurt the person. Sometimes jokes cease to be funny. What are you trying to prove? That you're a big person? By having a kick at someone else's expense? So that person may have hurt you, but does doing two wrongs make a right?

You're struggling. You can't run anymore. That's as much as you're going to lift today. I get it. You want to maximize your potential. You want to get stronger and faster. I understand. But how will you train if you get injured or damage yourself? Is that extra rep worth not being able to train properly for the next few months? It is better to have six fantastic runs that were executed with perfect technique than nine half-baked attempts.

How much more money do you need? You're already earning £300,000 a week. Some people don't even earn that in a lifetime, let alone in a week.

Yes, careers are short, and you do need to maximize your earnings. But money isn't the root of everything. What about glory? Can you really say that you won the title if you spent most of the time sitting on the bench? How do you want to be remembered? Do you want to be known as one of the best to have ever graced this sport, or do you want to be known as a money-grabbing mercenary? Money you can always earn, but titles you cannot.

Know your limits. Don't let greed rule you. If you have something good, protect it, enhance it. Don't necessarily go off and try to seek something better when you already have gold in front of you. The grass isn't always greener. Sometimes you need to know when you need to say enough is enough.

The Beautiful Game

Football is arguably the most popular sport in the world. A sport represented by the global body that is FIFA; an organization that at the time of writing has 211 membership countries. A sport that is played everywhere, from continent to continent to classroom to playground. Even in your living room you can have a quick game of football. It really is a global phenomenon. A sport that has captured the hearts of millions of people around the world. But what is it that makes football the beautiful game?

To begin with, you have the players. Everyone in some shape or form has witnessed some of the greatest players to have ever played the game. From legends of years gone by—such as Pele, Cruyff, Charlton, Best, Maradona, Moore, Platini, Van Basten—to modern-day greats such as Ronaldo, Messi, Neymar, Zidane, Figo, Brazilian Ronaldo, and Ronaldinho. Legendary players who have gone on to become heroes of folklore. These are players who have transformed the sport. Each took football to new heights and ensured the game will live on in people's hearts forever.

Look at some of the legendary matches. In the Premiership era, everyone will remember the Liverpool-Newcastle match in 1996. That match was a showcase for goals and attacking football galore. If you're a Manchester United fan, you will always remember the way they won the treble in 1999 against the German powerhouse in Bayern Munich. How about Brazil's legendary 4–1 victory against Italy in the 1970 World Cup final? Or the match in which Ronaldinho scored four goals against Real Madrid at the Bernabeu. These matches will be remembered forever.

Then you have the excitement of match day itself. The build-up, the banter, the anxiety, the expectation—all of it adds to the match day experience. We share the pain of losing and the glory of winning. There is nothing better than seeing your team win, especially if it is a last-minute winner. It is sheer ecstasy when your team wins.

In football, you have some of the most iconic sporting arenas, stadiums such as Wembley, Old Trafford, Anfield, Nou Camp, San Siro, Amsterdam Arena, Stade De France. These stadiums have witnessed some of the most historic and memorable moments in the game. These stadiums are pillars, tourist attractions in their own right. These stadiums act as beacons for all that is beautiful about football.

Anyone can play football. All you need is a ball and two items to act as goalposts. There is also something for everyone. If you have pace and trickery, you can play as a winger, ala Ryan Giggs, or a fast forward like Thierry Henry. If you have stamina, you can be a box-to-box player like Roy Keane or Patrick Vieira. If you like to use your hands, try the goalkeeping position. With luck, you could be the next Buffon or Peter Schmeichel. If you like to put in a good tackle, defence is where it's at. The Franco Baresi's and Paolo Maldini's of this world made defending an art form. Perhaps you have an eye for a pass. Classic no. 10s like Andrea Pirlo and Eric Cantona were masters of this. Anyone can get in involved and that just adds to the beauty of the game.

And then we have the goals. The aim of the game is to score more goals than your opponent. Right foot, left foot, header, penalty, and free kicks all count. Football has been blessed with some memorable goals. Beckham from the halfway line, Ryan Giggs tearing apart the Arsenal defence in the 1999 FA Cup, Maradona's winner against England in 1986, Paul Gascoigne vs. Scotland in Euro 1996. How about the classy touch and finish from Dennis Bergkamp against Argentina at the 1998 World Cup? Or the sublime technique from Zidane against Bayer Leverkusen in the 2002 Champions League final. The goals are the highlight of the beautiful game and the moments we wait for.

Over the years, there have been challenges to the beautiful game. For example, the corruption at FIFA with Sepp Blatter and company at the helm. The ever-increasing ridiculous amount of money spent on players that, in truth, are not even close to being worth that actual amount of money. The lack of young players breaking through to top-level football. More teams choosing to park the bus and play negative football. Racism is still prevalent in certain parts of the game. The various scandals, be it dodgy agents or child abuse. You could argue that football has lost some of its innocence.

You can argue that we sometimes take football too seriously. I mean, we travel all over the world to support our beloved teams, spending so much money, and it hurts when they let us down or produce performances that make us feel like they don't care. That's why people go nuts on platforms like ArsenalFanTV; it's because they care. Unfortunately for some people, football may be all they have; it's a form of escapism. It is important to remember that it is just a game. Whereas you're struggling to pay off a mortgage, most footballers can pay for their houses outright. There is more to life than football.

But let this not detract from what made us love football in the first place. When we first kicked a ball and pretended to be our favourite players, we weren't thinking about big money, fame, glory, or all the other stuff. It was about enjoying this great sport and everything it had to offer. It's about emulating the skills such as the Cruyff turn, bend it like Beckham, dribble like Giggs, or make overhead kicks Rivaldo style. That's why we play the beautiful game. As long as we remember the spirit of football, it will always and forever more remain the beautiful game.

Will the Real Brazil Please Stand Up?

Brazil, the greatest footballing nation on the planet. At the time of writing this book, Brazil have won the most World Cups. It is a country that truly represents what the beautiful game is all about.

Even Alan Hansen, a man known for being all about defence, loves watching Brazil. Nine times out of ten, Brazil is the team you want to watch at the World Cup. So what makes Brazil worth watching? For starters, let's look at the names that have donned that famous yellow jersey: Pele, Garrincha, Jairzinho, Socrates, Romario, Bebeto, Juninho, the original Ronaldo, Rivaldo, Ronaldinho, Roberto Carlos, Cafu, Kaka, and Denilson. I could go on and on. Brazil was as good as it gets.

So what happened? All of sudden, the samba style was done. The swagger, the style of play that brought us so many beautiful moments—such as Roberto Carlos's free kick against France in 1997, Ronaldo tearing through the opposition like an express train, Jairzinho's goal against Italy in 1970, Pele proving to the world in 1958 if you're good enough you're old enough, the baby celebration during that 3–2 win over Holland in 1994—was gone just like that.

Instead, I see a function-based game where a lot more emphasis is on physical strength and defensive rigor. Instead of the thousand stepovers Denilson used to do, I'm more likely to see a long punt. This isn't Brazil. These are imposters. I want my Brazil back. Will the real Brazil please stand up?

Perhaps the 1982 defeat against Italy hurt them more than we realized. Perhaps Brazil feels they can no longer win playing with that style and that samba is an outdated concept. But football isn't just about winning; it's about enjoying. The best football teams are not just the ones that win; they are the ones that play the game in the right way (Jose Mourinho take note).

The Manchester United sides of 1994, 1996, 1999, and 2008 didn't know the meaning of the word "defeat." The 2004 Arsenal Invincibles were a joy to watch. Spain from 2008 to 2012 rewrote the script on how to play the game. France from 1998 to 2000 was one of the most complete teams I have ever seen. How about the Ajax side from the 1970s and 1995? Or the great Messi/Guardiola-inspired Barcelona? But for me, none were the equal of the truly great Brazil sides such as the 1970 iteration.

Who knows, some day we may see that Brazil again. The one who used to be, as the Rock would say, "the most electrifying team on the planet." Perhaps a new generation will emerge and help Brazil get back the glory and style that made them famous. Maybe the Brazil we know and love will come again. Maybe one day the real Brazil will stand up. It will be a shame and big loss to the world if the samba way of playing football is truly lost.

Entitlement

I'm entitled to this. That job should be mine. We should be winning the Premiership as we have won it the most times. I should be winning the Olympic and world titles because I'm the best out there. On my day, there is no one who can beat me. I should have guys swooning all over me; they should be treating me like a princess and be lucky to be with me. Well, guess what? You're not entitled to anything. You have no divine right to get whatever you want, so get over yourself.

No one has a divine right to anything. In this life, you must work for and earn whatever you have, regardless of what it is. Okay, so you have been the team to beat previously. That doesn't mean you should automatically win it the next year. Your rivals are going to do everything they can to beat you, so you need to always be on your toes, looking to move forward. You can't take your eyes off the ball even for a second. You should always be looking to the future and never stand still.

You may technically be the best sprinter out there. You may have the world record. But that was just a one-off race. When it comes to the championship, it is about who performs on the day. Reputations mean nothing. You can't just turn up expecting to win. You've got to go out there and perform if you want to bring home the gold.

You may have many qualities that a man looks for in a woman. You're beautiful and intelligent. However, relationships are about give and take. If you want him to treat you like a princess, you have to show him you're worth it. You talk about wanting to be treated as equals, but you always expect him to pay for everything. You must put in your share as well. And the same goes for us guys as well.

In life, there is no such thing as a free lunch. If you want to be entitled to something, you have to work for it and prove that you're worth it. And not just prove it once but all the time. Earning a title is one thing. Keeping it is a totally different matter.

I Remember

I remember a time when, in the middle of an afternoon, I would go to the park and play outside for hours with my friends. There was no fear of kidnapping, no fear of paedophiles, and no fear of anything going wrong. It was just a case of kids being kids.

I remember when I was at school; the playground was exactly that, a playground. It was a chance to have a break from lessons and run-around like there is no tomorrow. You got into the odd scrap here and there, but that was just us boys being boys. You go to a playground now, and there are CTV cameras. Now you go to a playground, and sometimes the kids won't be playing. Now it seems it isn't cool to be sweating. Whatever happened to sweat being part of the fun?

I remember a time when my baby sister was still a fat, tiny baby. A baby who used to come up to me, tap me on my leg, and have her hands stretched out for carry. Picking her up and throwing her up in the air used to put a big fat grin on her face. Now she's a mature woman, chasing her own dreams and goals. Seeing her grow up so fast has been amazing.

I remember a time when 4-4-2 was the standard formation in football. Everyone had a number 9—an Alan Shearer, Les Ferdinand, Ian Wright, Andy Cole, Robbie Fowler, Ruud Van Nistelrooy—players who just wanted to stick the ball in the back of net. Everyone used to have a number 10—an Eric Cantona, Denis Bergkamp, Teddy Sheringham, Gianfranco Zola—to link the play. Defenders then just wanted to defend. Now 4-4-2 is seen as outdated. The world is not producing as many great number 9s anymore; they are few and far between. Now everyone wants to be a false 9, and defenders need to be comfortable on the ball. Park the bus; there used to be no such thing. Back then, it was simply a case of attack, attack, attack, attack, attack, attack.

I remember wrestling in the 1990s. I mean; you had The Rock, Stone Cold Steve Austin, Undertaker, Goldberg, the New World Order (NWO), Bret Hart, and Sting. The *Monday Night War* revolutionized professional wrestling. The matches back then were electric. Now when I see wrestling, I change the channel. I can't relate to it anymore.

There are a lot of things I can still remember. I remember graduating; I remember starting my first full-time graduate job. I remember the 1992 Olympics and Nigeria beating Spain 3–2 at the 1998 World Cup. I remember Manchester United winning the treble. Those were all good times. You always remember the good times. But it's no good just being stuck in the past. Times have changed. Things move on. You need to move with it. Also, you change, especially when you get older, and that's a good thing. If you were still doing the same things you were ten years ago, you haven't really learnt anything. It's important you grow and take on new things. That's the only way you will grow as a person.

Remember the good times. They are memories you will cherish for a lifetime. Embrace change, and make it work for you. Just remember to abide by your principles and values, and you'll be just fine. Now it's time to make some new memories.

Spending a Decade Here

Ten years: an entire decade. Wow. Where did all the time go? I still remember getting here as a fresh-faced graduate, ready to conquer the world. I've learned a lot in that time. So here's to a decade here and counting. And what I've been through in the past decade could be a book by itself. So here is the short version.

I remember when I first arrived here. I was the fresh kid on the block. I was the new guy with everything to learn and no time to lose. The one who spoke what was on his mind and didn't care what people thought. The one who took no prisoners.

Everything at first was plain sailing. I came in and delivered. It was a case of eat, sleep, accomplish, repeat. It was non-stop progress in pursuit of my dream. Opportunities came at home and abroad, and I gladly took them. Then all of a sudden, out of nowhere, the brick walls started appearing. Project circumstances bought unnecessary pains. Being on the receiving end of some bad criticism and at times being the scapegoat for things that were unfairly pinned on me.

Question marks appeared. Some wondered about me. Some questioned whether certain dreams were possible and whether my aspirations were realistic. Despite that, I soldiered on. I knew what my purpose was. I knew what I came here to do. Bit by bit I rebuilt myself. I tweaked my approach. I restored the aggression I felt I lost during my bad moments. I returned home and came back to the people I knew had my back and believed in me. Then finally, at long last, the first main promotion arrived. The title of associate had come. I remember how I felt after finally jumping the grade from analyst to associate. It was relief getting that monkey off my back. The initial humps were gone. A light bulb went off. I was about to go into fifth gear. I just didn't realize it.

Suddenly, things just clicked. The momentum had swung, and I went on to have my best year at the firm yet. The review that year was sensational. The funny thing is I didn't see that review coming. Sometimes just knuckling down and taking care of your business can bear fruit. Little did I know that the best was still to come.

My role subtly started to change. I was sneakily given two contractors to manage on our testing initiative being run at the time. At first, I hated it. I didn't come here to manage people. I'm a software engineer; I design, I architect, I implement, and I roll out. I really wasn't feeling it. But sometimes you need to roll with the punches and take your medicine. Down the road, you know you'll come out swinging.

A few months later, my manager approached me and an unexpected vacancy had arrived. In the space of five months, we lost both our U.I (User Interface) technical leads. I wondered what on earth was happening. The U.I was a space I had been heavily involved in; I felt my world was being turned upside down. We spoke about the situation, and he asked why don't I do it. My exact words to him were, "Are you mad? It's too risky." The problems I had in years gone by were still in the back of my mind. I felt he had to be kidding me. I had already been down a certain path, and it was a road I swore I would never take again.

I thought about his offer. I did a lot of thinking. Despite my reservations, I took on the role. Taking on your first senior role—a global one in fact—is never easy. At first, I wondered, *what am I doing here?* It was as if I was wearing the wrong trouser size; it was as if they were too big for me. Only five months before, when one of my predecessors as U.I lead departed, he told me I was not ready yet. And deep down, I knew it. Those words stung me. He even said that to get to certain positions in this firm required me to conform, and some people only make it by kissing up to managing directors. With all this to process, I managed to get through it. I was ready. I went on to succeed. So what changed? I did.

Instead of focusing on the title, I focused on the mission ahead of me. I figured if we were going to do this, we were going to do this right. So out came the meetings, out came the planning, and out came the architectural blueprints. It was time for this organization to see what my leadership was all about. It was time for our platform to go to the next level, and I knew

I was the man who could deliver it. It was time for me to make this role my own. The torch was about to be passed.

Then at one global meeting, our senior tech lead began by telling the others that I would be presenting the team's U.I strategy. Everyone listened and agreed with where I was coming from. Just like that, in a puff of smoke, the dark clouds had gone. It was clear. The kid had grown into the man. The mantle had officially been passed. I truly was the U.I lead. By the time the year was about to end, the firm gave me another title. I had ascended to the rank of vice president. A triumphant moment, or so you would think.

When I made associate, I was over the moon. When I became vice president that was not how I felt. Instead I felt anger and annoyance. I was like, *what is this?* A lot of people congratulated me. I had phone calls from two managing directors I had the utmost respect for. Another manager director pinged me via Instant Messenger, saying, "Yes, well done." My baby sister cried with happiness for me when I told her. Yet why did I feel these emotions?

Perhaps, despite my recent successes, the ghost of what happened to me in the early part of my career was still at the forefront of my thoughts. I returned after the Christmas holiday, thinking I'd just pretend the promotion to vice president didn't happen. For me, it was business as usual. On my first day back, my global team lead called me into a meeting. He had gotten wind of my concerns and gave me a telling off. He reminded me of all the work I had done to get to this point. He told me about the people who had supported me to get there and that I should embrace it. After all, he had been one of the people who really stuck his neck out for me and cleared certain barriers. I accepted the bollocking but not the title.

In my mind, I was the U.I lead; I didn't think of myself as vice president. For me, it was a title that was non-existent, despite what appeared on my firm's profile page. My view only changed during my vice president orientation. A senior partner of the firm said, "Enjoy it. This may be the only time you have your name appear on a publicly announced firmwide title." That's when it hit me. This wasn't just all me. I had people around me to get to this point. So I celebrated with the people around me.

I spent two glorious years as the U.I lead, and it was a pleasure doing that role. I embraced it wholeheartedly and did a lot during my time in that role. But all great things have to come to an end. I had been with the same team throughout my career. A king needs to know when it is time to step down and hand over the keys to someone else. It was time for mobility and to change teams. This wasn't a goodbye; it was a, "See you later, and thanks for everything." The skills and challenges I had taken on would serve me well and continue to allow me to grow further in my new role.

Ten years. It has passed by in a flash. I look around, and a significant portion of the people I started with are no longer here. Some of the people who used to be senior to me are now my peers. Job titles I used to aspire to one day I now have. Instead of being managed, I'm expected to manage. It's truly a circle of life moment. I've come full circle. And I did it my way. I didn't bow to anyone or conform to some preconceived image. If anything, it was because of my approach and style that I got to where I am.

After ten years here, I keep getting asked what it is that has kept me here. What still makes me wake up every morning to come in and do this? It's a question I asked myself last Christmas. One is hunger; there are still things that I want to accomplish. Second, it is growth. Some of the things that I have had the opportunity to do here I may not have gotten to do elsewhere. And last, because of the people. The people have made being here an absolute pleasure.

My story here isn't done. There is still more to accomplish. There are still a few stops on the mountain that I am yet to climb. I have no idea when this story will end. As far as I'm concerned, I'm still at the beginning. So here's to what the next few years or however long I'm here will bring. On that note, it's time for me to get back to work.

When Tomorrow Never Comes

There is a report that is due. I've nearly completed it. I'm almost there. I only have five hundred words to go. It's okay; I can do it tomorrow.

I have a job application to complete. It doesn't close till next week. I still have time to get it done. I can do it tomorrow.

I still have two more laps to go to finish this session. I'm training for a competition in three months. I still have time to get ready. It's all right; I'll do those last two laps in my next session. I can do it tomorrow.

I really want and need to buy that spare part for my car. It will only take ten minutes for me to place the order. But my car is still fully functional, so it can wait. It can wait till tomorrow.

I saw a house I really like. It has everything I want in a home. I can see myself building a future there. My family liked the house as well. I need to make a bid for the house. I don't feel like doing it now; it can wait till tomorrow.

All these are things we want to do but never do them. We think we have all the time in the world. We say that we will do it tomorrow, but then we put it off. We say we will do it the next day. Then the next day comes, and we put it off again. We put it off until the next day, and then the next day slips and the one after that and the one after that. Now we are in a vicious cycle of no return. Before you know it, the time has gone. The penny has slipped. The window of opportunity has gone, and we can't complete it any longer. Doing it tomorrow is no longer an option.

What about when tomorrow never comes? What about if you don't wake up tomorrow? What about if that job vacancy is no longer there? What about if someone else takes that post? How do you know the price of the part you want won't go up, and by the time tomorrow comes, it is no longer affordable? Or worse still, what about if your car breaks down when you really need it. Or you get stopped by the authorities for not doing the right thing on time.

What if someone else makes an offer on your dream home, and the chance to outbid them has gone. In terms of training, every session you skip out on, your competitors put in double shifts to make sure that when the time comes, they are ready. When you're so close to the finish line, why wait? Why not finish the job there and then? You can rest while you sleep. You can recover when you go and eat. But that moment—that moment when you have the edge, when you have the momentum—may never come again. Seize the moment; take the opportunity. You may never be in that position again. You never know what tomorrow will bring.

When you have the opportunity to do something, don't wait do it. This is your window; you're in the right place, right frame of mind and it's the right time to make something happen. Don't waste it. Don't wait for tomorrow. By then, it may be too late. Instead of letting tomorrow never come, let today be the day you get it done.

What Really Matters?

What is important to you? I'm serious. What are the things that are important to you? Money, you may say. Your house, your car, your job perhaps. Maybe it is the team that you support. Now let me ask you a different question. What really matters?

Interesting question, isn't it? All those things I suggested do matter. But the real question is to what degree they should matter. How important are they, and where should they be in terms of your list of priorities?

Money. We live in a world where we need money to do things. I needed money to write and get this book published, for instance. We need money to take care of our loved ones and do the things we want to do in life. However, that doesn't mean we should solely focus on getting the money and forget about everything else in life. It is important to have money, but don't let that be your sole purpose in life. Don't place money above spending time with your loved ones.

The house is important as we all need a roof to live under. The car helps us get places we would not be able to otherwise. But the thing to remember is these are material items. We can't take them with us once we depart this world. So don't forget to get out of the house. See your friends. Leave the car at home for once, and go for a run or walk. Enjoy the good weather when you can. Don't forget to enjoy the simple things in life.

As for our favourite teams/persons, sporting or otherwise, we all have our passions and things we enjoy. But let's not forget that it is only a game. It isn't life and death. There is more to this world than whether your favourite team or persons bring home the gold. So relax, and don't forget to embrace the real world.

So what does matter in life? It's a question of perspective, I suppose. Things that should matter are things you can't get back once they're gone.

Like your family and loved ones. Money and jobs come and go. Material things can be replaced. But your loved ones, family, and friends are ones of a kind and can't be replaced. So give them a call once in a while. Visit them when you can. Never take them for granted. Look after them the way they would look after you. Make sure you can look yourself in the eye and say you did right by them. Embrace all that life offers you. If you have the opportunity to travel or do once-in-a-lifetime things, make sure you take the opportunity. Life isn't about simply 9 to 5 and mortgage. Life is about living. So make sure you go out there and live it. That is what really matters.

The Beauty of Programming

Programming, programming, programming. Programming: the process of instructing computers to carry out commands. We have so much power at our fingertips. With just a few lines of code, I can create anything I can imagine. With just a few lines of code, I can create a brand-new super-game. In just a few lines of code, I can get that robot to pick up bricks. In just a few lines of code, I really can make anything happen. This really is a case of the pen being mightier than the sword.

Programming at its purest is an art form. Just like painting, a good program needs a lot of work. It needs affection, love, and care. In addition, it needs great attention to detail. You'll struggle a lot; at times, writing programs can make you want to tear your hair out. You'll make several alterations until you get it working the way you want it. But when it is done, what is left is a thing of beauty.

Programming: one of the few disciplines that can offer the best that science and engineering have to offer. You have the challenge of science in terms of discovering new ideas and techniques in addition to making something that is really your creation—exactly like you would in any other area of engineering.

In the world of programming, you can write code in many languages. It really is a case of take your pick. From Java to C#, JavaScript, Typescript, SQL, Perl, Groovy, Prolog, HTML, the world really is your oyster. It's like being in a candy store. Like candy, all languages have their sweet spots. And like candy, you can leverage them for different occasions. At other times, it may be a case of what do you fancy doing today?

Do you know what the best thing about programming is? It's the buzz. It's the thrill. It's that eureka moment, the moment of magic when it all comes together, and you finally have that program working. You can share your creation with the entire world via deploying it as a web application or making it available to install on user laptops and PCs. You can even make it available on someone's phone. It's the equivalent of scoring a goal in football. That sense of utopia can make you go crazy and make you want to celebrate like there is no tomorrow. All those late nights, all those hours spent scratching your head, debugging what went wrong, are forgotten in a moment. Programming is a thing of beauty. Do it right and then sit back, relax, and reap the benefits of what you wrote. Now let's run this code. It's time to press enter.

Why Computers Run the World

Computers are here, and they are here to stay. Computers are everywhere. Computers take various forms. Your mobile phone, laptop, high-tech stopwatch, and your Tom-Tom or other built-in car satellite navigation systems are all forms of computers. If there is a microchip inside it with a program running, it is a computer. Mini, Micro, Mac, Windows, Linux all need computers. What really runs the world? Well, right now it is computers.

Those coordinated traffic lights responding to a pedestrian button press or an approaching car at a cross section, guess what runs them? Computers. The traffic control system used to coordinate aeroplane fights, a computer is responsible for that. Even the menu options available on your microwave are driven by a minicomputer.

Look around; computers are all around you. You can't get away from them. Through computers, we have access to all kinds of information in seconds. Computers are a great invention. Computers are a revolution. Computers provide us with all sorts of jobs. Computers play a very big role in modern life. The trick is to not to let them be your life.

Computers may help us run the world; but that doesn't mean they should be the only things that exist in our lives. Sometimes we need to switch off in a while. Sometimes you need to take a breather. Go out for a walk; get some running in. Why not read a book or a newspaper once in a while? Just remember there is a world outside computers. Instead of Facebook or WhatsApp, why not go and actually see the person?

Computers are great and do a lot for us. Embrace them, utilise them, and get the most out of this brilliant, magnificent tool. Just remember we lived for many years without a computer. Computers are your ally and will help you. But they are no substitute for real friends and interaction. Now go out and enjoy some of the real world.

The Plan

The plan. What is it I plan to do? I plan to get a house, get married, and have kids. I plan to live happily ever after. If only life was so simple. In life, things often don't go according to plan. Even the best-laid plans can be derailed. Circumstances can change; people grow and become different. Sometimes a plan may lead to a positive or negative outcome we didn't expect.

Life isn't meant to be a straight line. It's a zigzag, a seesaw. We may know where we want to go, but it may require us to take a detour. But that's okay; life would be pretty boring if we knew exactly how everything was going to turn out. Plan ahead; Think about the future, but prepare for the unexpected. Life is a one-time adventure, so enjoy the ride whilst you can. You can still reach your destination. There's more than one way to skin a cat. It just may take a little longer than expected.

Sometimes you need to know when to throw out the plan and just take life as it comes.

I Wish

Imagine you had a genie who could grant you as many wishes as you desire. What would you wish for? It's a question I asked myself recently. I spent some time thinking about this, and here's what I came up with.

I wish I had the ability to time travel but not for the reasons you are probably thinking. A lot of people want to go back in time to change their pasts, to correct mistakes, or change things they did. I believe your past makes you who you are today but for me. I would like to time travel and relive some of the greatest moments of my life. Moments such as my graduation, passing my driving test, winning the 100m at Sports Day, witnessing the London 2012 Olympics, my first time visiting New York, seeing the Nou Camp up close, making the Robot Football project a reality. These are moments I would love to experience all over again. What made those moments so special is the journey involved in each of those moments. Life moves on so quickly, we sometimes forget to enjoy those moments. I wish I could enjoy the moment of each of those things again.

I wish for Manchester United to regain their sporting identity. The Manchester United I grew up watching was feared and admired in equal measure, playing swashbuckling attacking football along the way. Manchester United never knew when they were beaten. I wish for a return to the days of glory, glory Man United.

I wish for the day when CCTV is no longer required at school. I understand why they have it, but I remember school being a place for learning, having fun occasionally and being a central point of growing into a young adult. I wish we can someday let our children attend schools safely without the need for CCTV.

I wish the concept of marriage was respected more. Marriage is supposed to be for better or worse, till death do us part. It's about doing right by your family and thinking about others. Now it's as if people get married for show or just to have an excuse for an expensive do with fancy dresses. Sometimes people get married, and five minutes later, they get divorced. Did they not think it through? What were they looking for in the first place? I wish people would enter marriage with their minds clear, focused, and knowing what they want for the rest of their lives.

I wish I could fly into space just once. Reaching the moon was one of humankind's greatest achievements. Space, the final frontier; it really is a sight to behold. I would just love to view all stars and planets in their full glory one day. I'm sure it would be an experience I would never forget.

I wish for my friends and family to continue to grow peacefully and happily. They really have been beacons in my life. They have been with me every step of the journey and are always there when I need them. I love them all and wish them only the best.

But do you know what I wish for most? Peace and togetherness. The world is really divided at the moment. It's as if everyone is functioning in their own little worlds. I can't remember a period when the planet has been so divided. Things like Trump and Brexit are not helping. Why can't we all just get along? If I only had one wish, it would be to let us all live together in peace and harmony.

My Favourite Meal

Me, I love my food. I'm known to be a big eater. There are many meals that I enjoy. But my favourite is Jollof rice, chicken, and dodo (fried plantain). There's nothing like it. Yummy, yummy.

What's there not to like? You have the fulfilment of rice combined elegantly with the sweet succulent chicken or another meat of your choosing, the tomato mixed with the very best of spices, mixed in traditional West Africa style, with the sweet taste of dodo mixed in for good measure. Give me Jollof any day of the week.

What is it about this dish that does it for me? Personally, I enjoy the fact that I can eat it anytime and anywhere. Weddings, birthdays, lunchtime, or dinner; there is no occasion when Jollof rice is out of place. Anytime, anywhere, I'm always ready for a portion of Jollof rice.

The best part of this dish is that it is something everyone can enjoy. If you don't like chicken, you can make it with beef or goat. You don't like meat; you can make a vegetarian version. The only thing better than eating Jollof is eating it with other people. The food has been cooked, and it's time to sit down and eat. Enjoy!

Origins

Where are you from? That's a question we all get asked a lot. But how often do we give an honest answer? Sometimes we say we are from somewhere else. Why? Simply because we are afraid of how people will react. We are afraid of what people will think. Or worse still, we are ashamed of where we come from.

No country, area, or region is perfect. Every part of the world has its flaws. It's simply a case of certain flaws being more exposed than most. Regardless of where you're from, be proud of it. There is greatness everywhere. You just need to know where to look. There is a saying that "Despite your origins, you can do anything." I'd rather think that because of your origins you can do everything. Why? When you know where you come from, you know where you're going. You will know your worth, and nothing will deter you.

Your origins are your roots. They're your baseline; they're your seed. A tree cannot grow without roots. Strengthen these roots. They are the foundation upon which you build. Every good house needs a solid foundation. Never forget your roots. Never forget where you come from. Be proud of your origin; don't fight it. Recognize and embrace it. This will enable you to go from strength to strength. Your origin is with you for life. Remember that.

No One Ever Thinks to Ask the Question

I go past this spot every single day. It sure looks interesting. I wonder what is inside. Why not go up and ask what it is all about? Surely it is better than always wondering what is inside that building.

There is a person I like. I've had a huge crush on this person for a while. I wonder if the individual will like me back. Why not go up and ask? What's the worst that person can say? If you don't ask, you don't get.

I see this guy do the same drill all the time. Others try it, but no one executes it as flawlessly as he does. I wonder how he does it. Maybe I should ask him. There's no harm in asking, right? Who knows? You may pick up a new training technique.

I always wondered what he meant by that statement. He uses it so much in his lectures. I have never fully understood what he meant. So one day I asked him. I was really surprised at his answer. It really was a wow moment, one when it all made sense and clarified a lot of other questions I had. After the lecture, all my classmates came up to me and said they wished they asked that question sooner. Why is it no one ever thinks to ask the question?

Why Always Me?

Why always me? Why is it always me? Why am I the one who always ends up getting into trouble? I can be minding my own business, not saying a word, but I'm always the one who ends up in trouble. I'm the one who always gets into a fight.

Why always me? I'm a genuinely nice person, but when it comes to finding a partner, I always end up getting shafted. Nice person, yet they always end up with someone else. Why is it I'm the one who always gets turned down?

Why always me? I go into the major tournaments as the world no. 1. I'm the fastest person around, the one to beat. Yet when push comes to shove, I don't get the Big G. The gold ends up going elsewhere. Am I destined never to win a major title?

Why always me? I work my butt off. I work harder than everyone else. I put in more hours than the people who get promoted. Yet I don't get noticed. What do I need to get to the next level?

Why always me? That's a good question. Instead of asking that question, how about trying to answer that question. So you get in trouble a lot. Who do you hang around with? Are they the troublemakers? Do they have your back when things get rough, or do they leave you hanging dry? Maybe it's time to leave them hanging and be with people who are worth your time and will have your back come rain or shine. Your network is your net worth; never forget that.

So you're having issues finding a partner. So where are you looking? Is it always the same website? Is it always the same nightspot? Try widening your circle. Try different spots. Try different activities. The world is a big place, so why limit yourself? Insanity is doing the same thing over and over again and expecting a different result. You're not insane, are you? Try something new, and you may surprise yourself with what you end up with.

To get the best of yourself, you've got to know what makes you tick. If you're a fun person, have fun; relax. If you're a tense person, think and do things that remove the tension. It is easier said than done, but if you're always placing the world on your shoulders, you'll eventually fall under the weight of expectations. Take a deep breath, relax, and trust in your ability. Practice tunnel vision; block out everything else and just focus on what you need to do to perform. As for getting promoted, work smarter not harder. Look at the people who get promoted. Observe the traits they have and what they bring to the table. Speak to people who have been where you are. You'll get there. Just have faith.

Why always merit's a very good question. Human beings are arguably the biggest riddle of them all. Sometimes the answer can lie within. You get to an age where you know yourself better than anybody else. You know what you like and what you don't like. Once you understand and master that, the question of why always me will cease to be. When the time comes, you'll know what to do. The results will be spectacular when you figure it out.

Out of Time

Time. No matter how hard we try, time is the one thing we can't stop. Time waits for no one. We are in this world for a short time. Before you know it, it is all over. And by then, we are really out of time.

When we're young, we think we have all the time in the world. We think we can take it easy. We think we'll never have to worry about all the grown-up stuff. We think we'll stay young forever. But one way or another, time catches up to all of us.

In six months you have a set of exams that will help shape your destiny. You know you have a lot of work to do. There are dozens of practice papers you know you have to go through. There are a lot of topics that you need to cover. Yet you put off doing the groundwork. You say you'll do it the next day. That day slips. Then the next day goes. Days become weeks, weeks become months, and before you know it, the exam is here. And now you want to cram. Too little, too late. What were you doing for the past six months? If you didn't get the grade you wanted, you only have yourself to blame. If you had started when you should have, you wouldn't have run out of time.

You've discovered something you're really good at it. And it's something that you enjoy doing. A lot of scouts are looking at you. The chance to turn professional in this field may arise. The path is there for you. You should be out there, practicing and honing your craft every chance you get. Yet what did you do? You squandered your chance. You didn't take it seriously. You took it for granted. You had the opportunity to be something special. Now you're just another unfulfilled talent. All the opportunities you once had are no longer there. The scouts are no longer interested. The game has moved on. You simply ran out of time.

So you're 1–0 down with twenty minutes to play. Yet you play the game at a snail's pace. You don't force the issue and act like you don't care. Then, before you know it, the final whistle blows. You think it's all over. Well, it is now. Yes, it may only take a few seconds to score a goal, but the process of getting into a goal-scoring position takes a lot longer. How about giving it your all from the get-go? You may get lucky in the final few minutes. But if you're not careful, you'll end up running out of time.

I remember starting secondary school in September 1996, just after Euro 1996. The only thing on my mind back then was playing football. All of a sudden, I was sitting my GSCSEs. The next thing I knew, I was going to university to study computer science. Then ten years later, at the time of this writing, I'm about to celebrate ten years in my current firm. Time goes by in a flash. Think about all those experiences you went through. Think about the growth you went through during that period. But also think about the things that went wrong. Think about the things you wish you could've done differently. Perhaps there were things that happened during that period you regret. You can't change the past; that's done. Unless time machines suddenly become a reality, you can't change your history. What's done is done, but you can change your future.

Think about where you want to be in ten years. What kind of life do you want to be living? What personal, social, spiritual, and professional positions do you want to be in? Make sure you take those necessary steps and prepare yourself now. Don't wait; get on it now. You don't want to be wondering in ten years why you didn't lay the foundations. By then it really will be too late. You will have run out of time.

Don't leave it too late. Don't wait around forever. Do it now whilst you still have the opportunity. You don't want to think in years to come, *If only I did it differently*. By then it will be too late. In life, you get a certain window, a period when everything is setup to make the most of your gifts. This is when you can make things happen. Those windows don't come around often. So when they do, seize the moment. Don't wait till the window closes. By then, you really will be out of time.

Ego

Ego is one thing that can hold us back. Sometimes it gets the better of us over and over again. Sometimes we are afraid to admit that we need help. Sometimes we let our egos get in the way in our quest for glory.

You had a simple pass on. All you had to do was square it to him. Instead, you went for glory yourself, and you missed. Then they went down to the other end of the pitch and scored. How do you feel now? You thought about glory and forgot about the team. Players may be able to win games, but teams win titles. Remember that the next time there is a better option before you try to hog all the glory for yourself.

You knew there was someone else who could have done a better job on the task in question. You know your skills are better suited to other things. Instead of sticking to what you're good at, you bit off more than you could chew. Your cost your team time and money. Your ego got the better of you. There is nothing wrong with stretching yourself, but know your limits. Don't let your ego get in the way of common sense. You will have your time to shine when the time and opportunity are right.

Did you really need to buy that car? Did you really need to buy yet another house? I mean, you already have five cars and ten houses. What are you trying to prove? You only use one car most of time, and you're not even using the other houses. What made you buy them? It was your ego. You don't need many properties or cars to show how successful you've been. If you want to share your wealth with your family and loved ones, by all means, you have earned it. But don't go on an unnecessary ego trip. It won't make you happy and will only leave you feeling empty inside.

Don't let ego get in the way of your pursuit of glory. You're not alone. You don't have to carry everything on your shoulders. As strong and gifted as you maybe, you are still flesh and bone. A human being can only do so much. Now put aside your ego, and let others help you.

The Motherland

Africa, the motherland. A beautiful place. Lots of sun, land, and raw natural goodness. Where else in the world will you find so much natural beauty? From our beaches to our waterfalls to the mountains. If you want natural clean water and air, you can find it in Africa. You want the safari, you have to come to the motherland. And as for our food, it is absolutely delicious. From Jollof rice to Keke to pondered yam to fried plantain, we have something for everyone. The motherland is what it's all about. The motherland is where it's it.

There is a lot of good in Africa, yet on occasion, it is often viewed with such scorn. It's gotten to the point that some people don't like saying they're from Africa. It is true we do have some challenges, but no place is perfect. The Western world has its own challenges. For everything bad I can name many good things. For my country, Nigeria, I can always look fondly at winning the 1996 Olympics football tournament, beating Brazil and Argentina on the way. I still remember the beating we gave to Spain in 1998, when they had Raul, Morientes, and company. And look at some of the greatest players to have graced football. Zinedine Zidane, Patrick Vieira, George Weah, Didier Drogba, Samuel Eto, and Eusebio all have roots in Africa.

Outside of sports, Africa has given so much to the world, including Nelson Mandela, an inspiration to the world; Chinua Achebe, a bestselling novelist from Nigeria; Desmond Tuto, Nobel Prize–winner; and Shaka Zulu, one of the great African kings. The motherland has given so much to the world and will continue to do so. Never forget that, and always respect the motherland.

Africa has so much untapped and unfulfilled potential. We have a potential paradise on our hands. It is a utopia wanting to be unearthed. Recently I saw the *Black Panther* film, a film I would now put among my all-time favourites. Like a lot of black people, I really felt inspired by that film. The first black superhero movie since *Blade.* But it was also a film that showcased Africa as a beacon for the world. Many of us wondered why Wakanda couldn't exist for real.

What's stopping us from making a real-life Wakanda? What is stopping us from making this a reality for Africa? Is it a lack of materials? No. We may not have Vibranium, but we have oil, exotic fruits and plants, and many other natural resources that can only be found in Africa. Is it the lack of scientific geniuses? Look at the world. We have so many people of African origin in important positions in big companies setting and being examples. The problem is they had to do that away from home. When they go home, their skills are sometimes not appreciated, rewarded, or even encouraged. In some cases, it is all three.

As for government, it is true that we have a lot of corruption there, but the rest of the world has corruption as well. Look at the scandals that have affected the Western world. Bill Clinton and Monica Lewinsky, Sepp Blatter and the corruption at FIFA, the Russian drug scandal. Corruption exists everywhere, not just in Africa. The real issue is we need our governments to be run by people for people. Too often, unfortunately, they are concerned with their own profits.

What about a hero? Where is the real *Black Panther*? The motherland doesn't need a hero. The motherland needs its people to stand together. We need to combine forces and grow each other as people. We need to grow our communities and spread empowerment. Knowledge, skills, and education are what is needed. We can all be Black Panthers. We just have to believe and take the small steps. The Roman Empire wasn't built in one day, and neither will creating a utopia for the motherland. We have decades to catch up. But bit by bit, we can get there. It isn't Wakanda forever. It is the motherland forever. It is the motherland for life.

The End

The end, the end of the road, the end of a journey. That's it, it's finished. You're done. It's all over. Every story has a beginning, middle, and end. This is the end. I've done everything I can in this place. At this moment in time, I have nothing else to prove. There are no more mountains to climb. Game, set, and match. It's over. Or is it?

Is that it? Are you done already? Is this really the end? Who says you're done? When one door closes, another one opens. A new journey is upon you. New challenges arise. Perhaps it's time to set yourself some new goals. Why not take a risk and see how far a different path can take you? There may be one Mount Everest, but that doesn't mean it is the only mountain worth climbing.

The end will come to us all at some point. Nothing lasts forever. But until we take our final breaths, why limit ourselves. There will come a day when we are not as fast as we once were when we can't bench press or squat the way we once did, or we can't do the 9 to 5 daily slog anymore. That time will pass. But that doesn't mean it is the end of you. There's more to you than your job, how much you can lift, or what you drive. This isn't the end. It's time to make a new ending. This isn't an evolution; this is a revolution.

This isn't the end. Your time isn't up just yet. Now on your feet, it's time to make a new ending.

9 781546 294504